GROWING YOUR LEADERSHIP

Other Titles by Wanda S. Maulding Green and Edward E. Leonard

A Field Book for Higher Education Leaders: Improving Your Leadership Intelligence (Rowman & Littlefield Publishers, January 2018)

Improving Your Leadership Intelligence: A Field Book for K–12 Leaders (Rowman & Littlefield Publishers, September 2017)

Leadership Intelligence: Navigating to Your True North (Rowman & Littlefield Publishers, September 2016)

The Soft Skills of Leadership: Navigating with Confidence and Humility, 2nd Edition (Rowman & Littlefield Publishers, November 2019)

Soft Skills for Leaders: Scenarios from Higher Education Administrators, Volume 2 (Rowman & Littlefield Publishers, December 2019)

GROWING YOUR LEADERSHIP

Scenarios from Practicing K–12 Principals, Volume 2

Wanda S. Maulding Green
and Edward E. Leonard

ROWMAN & LITTLEFIELD
Lanham • Boulder • New York • London

Published by Rowman & Littlefield
An imprint of The Rowman & Littlefield Publishing Group, Inc.
4501 Forbes Boulevard, Suite 200, Lanham, Maryland 20706
www.rowman.com

6 Tinworth Street, London SE11 5AL, United Kingdom

British Library Cataloguing in Publication Information Available

Library of Congress Cataloging-in-Publication Data Available
Library of Congress Control Number: 2019951812

ISBN: 978-1-4758-4964-6 (pbk. : alk. paper)
ISBN: 978-1-4758-4965-3 (electronic)

∞™ The paper used in this publication meets the minimum requirements of American National Standard for Information Sciences—Permanence of Paper for Printed Library Materials, ANSI/NISO Z39.48-1992.

CONTENTS

PREFACE ix

INTRODUCTION xiii

SITUATIONAL JUDGMENT TESTS xvii

CHAPTER 1: LESSONS IN CREDIBILITY 1

So Many Problems, So Little Time 3

Searching for Answers 4

Principle I: Simplicity 5

The Digital Age 7

Christmas Cheer? 8

Safety First 9

CHAPTER 2: CONTRIBUTING AUTHOR'S OPTIONS FOR CREDIBILITY SJTS 11

CHAPTER 3: LESSONS ON COMPETENCE 15

Changing School Dynamics 17

To Serve or Not to Serve 18

To Err Is Human 19

Meet the Press 20

It's Lonely at the Top 22

Little Miss Sunshine 23

Charmin Soft? 24

Unable to Walk the Line 25

Bloody Mess—Part I 26

Bloody Mess—Part II 27

CHAPTER 4: CONTRIBUTING AUTHORS' OPTIONS FOR COMPETENCE SJTS 29

CHAPTER 5: LESSONS ON ABILITY TO INSPIRE 33
Crunch Time 35
One for the Road? 36
Keeping Your Promise 37
Domestic Violence—Part I 38
Domestic Violence—Part II 39
Popular Request of a Different Kind 40
A Prom Dilemma 41

CHAPTER 6: CONTRIBUTING AUTHORS' OPTIONS FOR ABILITY TO INSPIRE SJTS 43

CHAPTER 7: LESSONS ON VISION 47
Dropping an "F" Bomb 49
School Is Never Boring 50
Insubordination? 52
Where Do We Go from Here? 53
Just Kid's Play? 54
About That Move 55

CHAPTER 8: CONTRIBUTING AUTHOR'S OPTIONS FOR VISION SJTS 57

CHAPTER 9: LESSONS ON EMOTIONAL INTELLIGENCE/SOFT SKILLS 61
Demonstrations and Recriminations 64
First Meeting Drama 65
A Bus Driver's Quandary 66
Paying the Price 67
Welcome to America 68
Gone Too Soon 69
By Popular Request 70
Bye Bye Birdie 71

CHAPTER 10: CONTRIBUTING AUTHORS' OPTIONS FOR EMOTIONAL INTELLIGENCE SJTS 73

CONTRIBUTING AUTHORS' SOLUTIONS FOR SJTS 77

CONTRIBUTING AUTHORS' SOLUTIONS: CREDIBILITY 79

CONTRIBUTING AUTHORS' SOLUTIONS: COMPETENCE 83

CONTRIBUTING AUTHORS' SOLUTIONS: ABILITY TO INSPIRE 89

CONTRIBUTING AUTHORS' SOLUTIONS: VISION 93

CONTRIBUTING AUTHORS' SOLUTIONS: EMOTIONAL INTELLIGENCE/SOFT SKILLS 97

APPENDIX A—SMALL GROUP CARDS 103

APPENDIX B—LEADER ACUMEN INTERPRETATION CHART 105

APPENDIX C—LEADERSHIP ORIENTATION 107

APPENDIX D—FUN AT WORK 109

APPENDIX E—SELF-KNOWLEDGE 111

APPENDIX F—ACTIVITIES TO IMPROVE YOUR LEADER ACUMEN 115

NOTES 119

ABOUT THE AUTHORS 123

ABOUT THE CONTRIBUTORS 125

PREFACE

In preparing to compose a new preface for this second volume of *Growing Your Leadership: Scenarios from Practicing K–12 Principals*, the original preface was reread numerous times. The end result of those readings was that we still felt that the preface captured the essence of what we wanted to say with some additions based on current commentary and research. Those additions are addressed in the new portion of the preface contained in the third paragraph.

One of the key points in *The Soft Skills of Leadership: Navigating with Confidence and Humility*[1] is that the soft skills that comprise the major leader acumen imperatives of credibility, competence, inspirational ability, vision, and emotional intelligence/soft skills can be learned. Leaders, aspiring leaders, or anyone who wishes to build their leadership capacity, with proper exposure and practice, can learn new skills or enhance skills they already possess. Learning or enhancing skills builds a leader's adaptive capacity. In *Geeks and Geezers: How Era, Values, and Defining Moments Shape Leaders*, Warren Bennis and Robert Thomas (2002) shared,

> To the extent that any single quality determines success, that quality is adaptive capacity. . . . When we look at who becomes a leader, we see enormous variance in IQ, birth order, family wealth, family stability, level of education, ethnicity, race, and gender. Certainly, these factors cannot be dismissed entirely. But in studying both very young and older leaders, we found over and over again that much more important than a person's measured intelligence—to take just one factor—was his or her ability to transcend the limits that a particular IQ might impose. In the case of intelligence, this includes avoiding the trap of seeing oneself as highly intelligent, hopelessly average, or below average to the exclusion of other, more useful self-definitions. We emphatically agree with Ford's Elizabeth Kao that "everyone has their own wall to climb." And we believe that both the willingness to climb those walls and the ability to find ways to do so are the real measure of a leader.[2]

Bennis and Thomas go on to say that leaders "learn important lessons, including new skills that allow them to move on to new levels of achievement and new levels of learning. This ongoing process of challenge, adaptation, and learning prepares the individual for the next crucible, where the process is repeated. Whenever significant new problems are encountered and dealt with adaptively, new levels of competence are achieved, better preparing the individual for the next challenge."[3]

Summarizing the concept of adaptive capacity in later writing, Bennis reemphasized the importance of adaptive capacity saying, "The ruling quality of leaders, adaptive capacity, is what allows true leaders to make the nimble decisions that bring success."[4] Making correct decisions is based on three premises: knowledge of a given situation, technical (hard/competency-based) skills, and (soft) people skills. Knowledge of events will vary from situation to situation, but a leader cannot succeed without the people skills that allow him or her to fully utilize his or her technical skills. It is the recognition of the importance of acquiring the technical and people skills and moving to acquire and/or enhance those skills as new discoveries or innovations occur or when new strategies develop that is the cornerstone of building leader acumen that allows a leader's adaptive capacity to flourish.

Current commentary and research continue to emphasize the importance of adaptive capacity or the ability to accommodate change. Additionally, that expectation has been expanded to include the ability of an organization to be adaptive as well as the individual leader. John Chambers, the chief executive officer of CISCO, a leading worldwide technology firm, has this to say about adaptive capacity or the ability to accommodate change: "I think now most CEOs would agree. If they don't change, they get left behind." He further contends, "She or he has to think much more outside the box. They have to reinvent themselves. They have to reinvent their company."[5]

Leaders must adapt and so must the organization they lead. According to Uhl-Bien and Arena (2018), "Leadership for organizational adaptability calls for scholars and practitioners to recognize organizational adaptability as an important organizational outcome, and enabling leadership (i.e., enabling the adaptive process through adaptive space) as a critical form of leadership for adaptive organizations."[6] And that enabling leadership "addresses how leaders can position organizations and the people within them to be adaptive in the face of complex challenges."

Moreover, Uhl-Bien and Arena share that "organizations and those within them to be flexible, agile and adaptive in response to changes associated with a volatile and often unpredictable world." The CEO, Chambers, and the researchers Uhl-Bien and Arena come to the same conclusion as Bennis and Thomas that adaptive capacity is vital to individual and organizational success.

Growing Your Leadership: Scenarios from Practicing K–12 Principals, Volume 2 takes the reader through a series of situational judgment tests (SJTs) that address the soft people skill areas that lead to success. The SJTs are drawn from real-life experiences and are testament to the challenges, large and small, that a leader faces and the leader acumen and adaptive capacity a leader must exercise to make correct decisions.

However, there is one difference between the SJTs in volumes 1 and 2. The authors (Maulding Green and Leonard) developed the SJTs in volume 1 from their own individual experiences. The SJTs in volume 2 come from K–12 practitioners who are either still active in the field or recently retired. Developing or enhancing your leader acumen and adaptive capacity and thereby your ability to make proper decisions is a foundational leadership ability. *Growing Your Leadership: Scenarios from Practicing K–12 Principals, Volume 2* takes you on a leadership development journey.

INTRODUCTION

THE CONCEPT OF LEADER ACUMEN

Leader Acumen is defined as "a construct that represents the level of leadership capacity an individual possesses at any given time. It addresses the leadership imperatives of credibility, competence, ability to inspire, vision, and emotional intelligence/soft skills."[1] Each of these leadership imperatives is subdivided into knowledge, skills, and dispositions as shown in the following table. Each of the imperative subscale items lends itself to defining the major category.

Credibility In 500 feet, stay right	*Competence Recalculating*	*Inspiration Satellite reception lost*	*Vision You have arrived at your destination*	*Emotional Intelligence Route guidance suggested*
Ethics or Personal Accountability	Discernibility	Enthusiastic	Commitment	Resilience
Honesty	Perception	Energetic	Sense of Direction	Communication and Listening
Responsibility	Conflict Resolution Skills	Passionate	Professionalism	Happiness
Trust	Problem-Solving and Decision-Making Skills	Optimistic	Decisive	Personality Traits
Integrity	Relationship Building	Genuine	Work Ethic	Sense of Humor
Sincerity	Planning and Implementation	Courageous	Concern for the Future	Assertiveness
	Assessment and Evaluation			Flexibility
				Empathy/Interpersonal Interactions

(Maulding Green and Leonard, 2016, p. 19).[2]

In the work *The Soft Skills of Leadership: Navigating with Confidence and Humility* is an assessment for individuals regarding the imperatives; this assessment is referred to as the Leader Acumen assessment. It includes the subscale items listed in the foregoing table. Ideally, the best starting point for using this field book is to take the *LEA Assessment*, if you have not yet done so. The assessment is available free of charge online at https://www.leadershipimprinting.com/.

This is a self-assessment and it is vitally important that you are absolutely candid in your responses. The results of the assessment will give you a snapshot of your leadership capacity. It is important for the test taker to acknowledge, however, that the assessment is a fluid one. You may take it today after a great day at work and reveal a higher score than you might, for instance, if taken when you have had many difficult days as a leader.

For a broader look at your leadership capacity, the authors suggest that you conduct a 360 evaluation (alternately referred to as a Circle assessment) by having people you work with, those who evaluate you, or those who work *for* you complete the survey. Conducting a 360assessment to accompany your self-assessment will provide you with a measure of the match or congruence of your view of your leadership capacity with the view of others directly associated with you as a leader or aspiring leader. You may do this by inquiring on the website via the "Contact Us" page at https://www.leadership imprinting.com/. Based on the results of your self-assessment and/or your 360 assessment, you are ready to work through the *Growing Your Leadership: Scenarios from Practicing K–12 Principals, Volume 2.*

However, taking the assessment is not required to make good use of the field book. The scenarios provided in the field book are a source from which to develop insight into and familiarity with the real-life situations with which K–12 educational leaders or leaders in general deal. Most any of the events described in the field book could and do happen to any leader (perhaps in a slightly different context). Leaders share many commonalities in terms of the issues with which they must deal, especially the soft skill/people-related issues.

HOW TO USE THE FIELD BOOK INDIVIDUALLY

Use of the field book is straightforward and simple. There are thirty-three scenarios based on the five constructs of Leader Acumen. All of the scenarios are K–12 education-based but are potentially adaptive to other leadership situations.

Select a scenario. Read the scenario carefully. Think about the situation described and the possible solutions. Jot down in the space provided the solution you think would lead to the best outcome for the scenario. Then jot down a rationale for your solution.

After you have completed this part of the activity, turn to the end of the chapter where the *Authors' Options* are located. Read the options carefully and choose a best response from those listed. (Note, each scenario lists a final option that is blank. If you believe your solution is better than those provided by the authors, you should pencil your solution in at this time.)

With your solution and rationale in hand and your choice from the *Contributing Authors' Options* list (or your own solution), turn to the section of the field book titled *Contributing Authors' Solutions* for SJTs to reveal the authors' solution* to the SJT (these are listed by chapter and scenario). Compare your solution and rationale to the *Contributing Authors' Solutions.* Close alignment of your solution and rationale with that provided suggests a well-honed sense of analysis of the situation. It is important to realize, though, that while some solutions and the accompanying rationale are better than others, there is often more than one acceptable way to resolve an issue/situation.

As a last step to gain further insight, the authors encourage you to read the complementary reading from *The Soft Skills of Leadership: Navigating with Confidence and Humility* and the relevant, contemporary selected related readings listed at the end of each scenario. Follow this same cycle as you read/work through the field book.

HOW TO USE THE FIELD BOOK WITH GROUPS OR INSTRUCTIONALLY

Using the field book as an instructional tool follows the same general pattern as for individual use with some differences. Divide the class into small groups. Provide each group with the SJT scenario. Instruct the group members to read the scenario carefully, think about the situation described and the possible solutions, and jot down individually in the space provided how they would respond to the scenario. Then jot down a rationale for the solution.

After each individual has completed this part of the activity, the facilitator should direct the groups to the end of the chapter where the *Contributing Authors' Options* are located. Individually, again, the class members should choose a best response from those listed. (Note, each scenario lists a final option that is blank. If the student believes his or her solution is better than those provided by the authors, he or she should pencil it in at this time.)

Next, time should be allowed within the small groups to share their choices and come to group consensus on the best solution. Time should also be allowed for discussion and dialogue regarding the rationale for the individual choices. (Prior to class, instructors should prepare answer-sharing cards to be utilized for this part of the activity. See Appendix A for an example.) After ample small group discussion time has been given, the instructor should ask the small groups to *raise the card* with the letter of the solution they have chosen.

The instructor should then guide the large group instruction regarding the choices the small groups have made with ensuing dialogue. All of this rich discourse is intended to help *grow* participants "adaptive capacity" for leadership. Additionally, the instructor may choose to share the *Contributing Authors' Solutions* with rationale along with rationale for rejection of the other choices. Repeat the process for each SJT scenario.

Whether used individually or in a group setting, the use of SJTs adds an element of realism to the concepts presented. SJTs also allow the reader to utilize his or her analytic skills and judgment in synthesizing a solution and rationale. Each of these is needed in a leadership situation as any decision can and, in all likelihood, will be examined and criticized and a leader must be able to defend his or her decisions.

An additional and equally helpful step is to require class members to select a mentor for the duration of the term. Prior to each face-to-face meeting, assign an SJT for review and discussion. Have individual members work through the SJT with the mentor. When the class reconvenes, move directly from review of the scenario to small group dialogue regarding mentor/mentee interaction/solution. After small group discussion, reveal answer choice options for consensus among the group.

Finally, to fully solidify the learning from the class, the complementary reading from *The Soft Skills of Leadership: Navigating with Confidence and Humility* is listed at the end. Additionally, relevant, contemporary selected related readings are presented at the end of each scenario to solidify the learning gained through practice. We have found that requiring the participants to prepare a reflective writing helps them to internalize the ideas and solutions and is fruitful toward the desired end product of leadership growth.

HEADED IN THE RIGHT DIRECTION?

The conceptual model for *Leader Acumen* is a GPS. With that framework in mind, there are many "directions" you might take to get to a final destination. As such, you may review your *Leader Acumen Assessment* and determine to work on the area where your score was lowest. That is fine. For example, you might skip over to the chapter with VISION-growing scenarios if that works best for you. The field book was designed for use individually if desired.

If you are an instructor, working with a class, the quickest route to your destination might be to work through from the beginning to the end. On the other hand, you might want to vary the scenarios to accommodate everyone in your class, rather than going through each topic before moving to the next. For you, getting to your destination might include waypoints along the route.

For all, the main thing to remember is that there are many ways to get to a specific destination. There is more than one correct way to solve a problem, and the quickest route to a solution may not always be the wisest. As you work through the scenarios, you will gain confidence in your navigational skills and become a better leader along the way.

SITUATIONAL JUDGMENT TESTS

Situational Judgment Tests (SJTs) are assessments where the test taker is presented with a real or hypothetical situation and is then asked to select the most appropriate response to that scenario. SJTs have been around since the early 1920s. They have been used for garnering feedback of those from managerial positions in the workplace to decision-making ability in the military.[1] Over the years, they have proved to be good predictors of job performance. The authors believe SJTs are a good tool to use, especially for a book of the nature of this one because as McDaniel and Whetzel put it, they (SJTs):

- have low adverse impact,
- assess soft skills,
- have good acceptance by applicants,
- assess job-related skills not tapped by other measures, and
- assess "non-academic, practical intelligence."[2]

With those considerations in mind, the situational judgment test is an excellent tool to use when growing one's skill set in *Leader Acumen*. As stated above, the typical format of a situational judgment test is for a brief scenario to be shared with the learner. Of course, this sharing may be done via video clip, live via role-play, or in a written form. After the student acknowledges the situation, typically, they are given multiple-choice responses to review and then select from. In this book, an additional step is added.

Prior to exposure to the *contributing authors'* multiple-choice answer options, the student is allowed to pen his or her own brief response to the scenario. This is done to allow the opportunity for rapid processing of *typical* thought processes: "What would I do in this situation without suggestion from others?" It allows the reader to reflect on his or her own "gut-level" response before being guided. This step, the internalization of an individual's usual/typical response, is critical in the growth aspect of this learning process.

It is important, then, for the reader to respond in the provided space as quickly and as honestly as possible. The reader should not be asking, "how *should* I respond" but rather, "how have I responded to a similar problem in the past" or even "what do I think is the best way to respond?"

For the classroom teacher, instructor, or workshop facilitator, SJTs have the best outcomes when the situation is presented to an individual (or group of individuals) via "live" mechanisms, that is, role-play, video cast, or podcast. However, they are still effective when shared only in written form. Traditionally, SJTs come in a variety of formats and responding mechanisms. Some are developed requiring the participants to rank order the stated options; others ask the participants to give only the *best* answer, yet others call for the *unacceptable* responses. For the most part, the SJTs included in this book ask for the participant to give the best response.

Additionally, the contributing authors have (at the end of the book) given the *Contributing Authors' Solutions* to the SJTs (whether correct or incorrect) a best response with a rationale for that decision and similarly have given rationales for the other choice options. The most important takeaway for these exercises is to help the reader hear a range of potential responses to a situation and most importantly, for the participants, over time, to become reflective learners.

The richness of these assessments comes from the facilitation of an invested leader into and through individual, small-group, and large-group sharing and interaction. It is through these mechanisms that the best and most rapid learning can take place. Supporting readings from the companion book, *The Soft Skills of Leadership: Navigating with Confidence and Humility*, follow each scenario but should not preempt the SJT itself. Additionally, selected relevant, contemporary related readings are presented at the end of each scenario to solidify the learning gained through practice.

SJTs were selected as the primary tool to help a student grow his or her own *Leader Acumen*. These learnings, as shared in *The Soft Skills of Leadership: Navigating with Confidence and Humility*, take time and repetitive activity to establish as norms as they are acquired in the most basal or primary parts of our brains.

1

LESSONS IN CREDIBILITY

One of the things that people notice about a leader, possibly more than any other thing a leader does, is the extent to which his or her actions are consistent with his or her articulated position. Followers are asking and answering (to their own satisfaction) a vital question about the leader. Does he or she say what he or she means and support that with his or her actions? The answer to that question defines the credibility of the leader.

The scenarios in this chapter are, in one way or another, related to a leader's credibility. If your Leader Acumen assessment scores indicated this as an area for needed growth, you should work through the scenarios with a couple of things in mind. First, as you work through the scenarios in the chapter, take particular note of the *Contributing Authors' Options* to each problem at the end of each chapter of SJTs. In working through the scenarios and reviewing the *Contributing Authors' Options*, one of the two things will happen. You will find disparity between your responses and the authors, or you might, indeed, find that your responses coincide with the authors' (see Appendix B for a graphic representation). Next, reflect on the information you gained from the Leader Acumen assessment. If you acknowledge that Credibility is an area for growth based on the assessment, ask yourself if this was based on your Self assessment, the Circle assessment, or both.

If either or both assessments (the Self or Circle) indicate that you have room for improvement in the area of leader Credibility *and* you are also finding disparity in yours and the *Contributing Authors' Options*, chances are you will find growth via working through these exercises and accompanying readings. However, be reminded, this will not happen overnight. Growing your *Leader Acumen* is a worthy endeavor but is a painstakingly time-consuming undertaking. It requires rewiring of your thought processes regarding learnings that are very ingrained into your most innate understandings and this takes time (see Appendix B for a graphic representation).

On the other hand, if you find your solutions and the solutions offered in the *Contributing Authors' Options* coincide highly, yet your Self score is lower than the means for the group shown at the end of your assessment for Credibility, one of the two things is happening. Either you are lacking in self-confidence, yet your decision-making is solid; or conversely, perhaps you are somewhat overconfident but nonetheless making good decisions. If the first is the case, working through the scenarios should enhance your self-confidence. The second option (overconfidence) is the one to be most wary of. Leaders in this category many times find themselves derailed as leaders, even though they generally are good decision makers. Working through the scenarios should help to instill the idea that there is more than one acceptable solution to most problem/issues and thus lessen one potential major consequence of overconfidence, feeling that you have the only viable solution.

If you opt to have a Circle/360 assessment done and find that your solutions and the solutions offered in the *Contributing Authors' Options* coincide highly, yet your Circle scores were outside the standard deviation (available from the LEAD team when a Circle/360 assessment is done) for Credibility, it is possible that a different set of problems is occurring. Either you are selecting the course of action you believe is best for the scenario, yet in reality you would not implement it, or the problem may be one of *perception*. It is much more likely that it is the former. Only in rare instances would the latter be the case. However, we insert it here for thought because, on occasion, it is the case. And, as the old saying goes, "Perception is reality."

Perhaps you are indeed highly credible, yet *perception* is the issue for your low scores in Credibility. This could be a case of projection. For example, you may not "look" credible and perhaps for legitimate reasons. You will recall from the chapter on credibility in *The Soft Skills of Leadership: Navigating with Confidence and Humility* (2nd edition), mention was made of how "what you wear" infers or projects an image. Such could be the case in this instance.

Finally, improving your leader acumen and "adaptive capacity" as stated in the preface, is a process. As you will recall, the notion of leader acumen is predicated on the theory that there is a genetic predisposition toward leadership.

As Marquis and Tilcsik[1] so aptly noted, imprinting may take place, during brief sensitive periods of high susceptibility during the formative process, during the teachable moment, or another yet different time of susceptibility; and that imprints once established are persistent.

The lessons in this book are to be utilized to grow Leader Acumen in this third way—over the long, repetitive process. To that end and to truly be imprinted with any of the competencies, actions for building the various skill sets may be found in Appendix F.

True Credibility is only gained by congruence of words and actions.

SO MANY PROBLEMS, SO LITTLE TIME

A parent calls with a concern that a student at your school is harassing their daughter. You are alarmed because this is the first you have heard of the situation. As you record the notes from the parent, you get specific times, dates, and names of people who could be involved or have been witnesses of the issues described by the parent. At the completion of the call, you assure the parent that you take their concerns seriously and you tell them that you will call them at the end of the day when you have had time to investigate their concerns. You begin your investigation while also attending to the Friday pep rally, lunch duty, and two other disruptive students who have to be removed from class. You are able to gather enough information to make a determination as to whether a particular student is guilty of having harassed this young student whose parent you spoke to earlier in the day. You are exhausted, and you have to get to the away football game you are covering that evening.

What do you do?

____

____

____

____

____

____

____

Suggested Reading: Maulding Green, W., and Leonard, E. (2019). *The Soft Skills of Leadership: Navigating with Confidence and Humility*, 2nd ed., Chapter 3. Lanham, MD: Rowman & Littlefield.

Additional Selected Reading: Hewlett, S. A. (2016). "The Attributes of an Effective Global Leader." *Harvard Business School Cases*, 1.

SEARCHING FOR ANSWERS

A high school student is identified as having prescription pills on campus. The student is searched as well as the student's locker and nothing is found. The student drives onto campus each day (as opposed to being a bus rider). When asked, the student gives permission for his vehicle to be searched. A grinder is found in his vehicle (marijuana paraphernalia).

What do you do?

____

____

____

____

____

____

____

Suggested Reading: Maulding Green, W., and Leonard, E. (2019). *The Soft Skills of Leadership: Navigating with Confidence and Humility*, 2nd ed., Chapter 3. Lanham, MD: Rowman & Littlefield.

Additional Selected Reading: Isaac, M. S., and Grayson, K. (2017). "Beyond Skepticism: Can Accessing Persuasion Knowledge Bolster Credibility?" *Journal of Consumer Research*, *43*(6), 895–912. doi:10.1093/jcr/ucw063.

PRINCIPLE I: SIMPLICITY

The professional educator accepts personal responsibility for teaching students character qualities that will help them evaluate the consequences of and accept the responsibility for their actions and choices. We strongly affirm parents as the primary moral educators of their children. Nevertheless, we believe all educators are obligated to help foster civic virtues such as integrity, diligence, responsibility, cooperation, loyalty, fidelity, and respect for the law, for human life, for others, and for self.

The Code of Ethics for Educators was developed by the distinguished Association of American Educators Advisory (AAE) Board and by the Executive Committee of AAE.

Principle 1 is described in the following:

1. The professional educator deals considerately and justly with each student and seeks to resolve problems, including discipline, according to law and school policy.
2. The professional educator does not intentionally expose the student to disparagement.
3. The professional educator does not reveal confidential information concerning students, unless required by law.
4. The professional educator makes a constructive effort to protect the student from conditions detrimental to learning, health, or safety.
5. The professional educator endeavors to present facts without distortion, bias, or personal prejudice.

You have been an assistant principal for four years. The principal at your school is assigned to a new school. Therefore, a new principal has been assigned to your school. The year is going well, and you think the principal has some good ideas. However, one day you are asked to do something that you feel is unethical and an invasion of privacy.

An irate parent calls you regarding dismissal from the previous day. A male student told her twin daughters that he was going to decapitate them by cutting their heads off with a knife while they were sleeping. This student has a very troubled home life as well as past behavioral problems.

The new principal is not on campus but has instructed you to contact her if anything unusual arises. You inform the principal via text of the issue and your solution (counselor visit and parental conference). District protocol requires a counselor meeting if a student threatens to harm themselves or others. Additionally, electronic documentation of the incident is mandated. The child admits saying the remark to the twin girls.

The documentation system has a section for counselors. The counselors are the only people who can see and enter the notes in this system. The student met with the counselor and notes were entered on this day. You receive a text from your principal informing you to suspend the child and attach all counseling notes. The child's notes could possibly have details about the child's home life and documented abuse, which the child has confided in the counselor in previous years.

As a member of the district's Superintendent's Suspension Appeals Committee, you are aware that doing so will divulge years of confidential notes between the child and counselor to everyone on the Appeals Committee as well as create visibility online for any teacher, administrator, and for his parents to read. The counselor completely disagrees and says those notes have been taken for years and are confidential.

What do you do?

____

____

____

____

____

____

____

Suggested Reading: Maulding Green, W., and Leonard, E. (2019). *The Soft Skills of Leadership: Navigating with Confidence and Humility*, 2nd ed., Chapter 3. Lanham, MD: Rowman & Littlefield.

Additional Selected Reading: Cooper, David J., Hamman, John, and Weber, Roberto A. (2016). "Fool Me Once: An Experiment on Credibility and Leadership." Retrieved from https://ssrn.com/abstract=2832372 or http://dx.doi.org/10.2139/ssrn.2832372.

THE DIGITAL AGE

A student posts a graphic statement about rape, torture, and murder on his Facebook page. Police notify school officials of the graphic statement. Though the student's personal social media rant was not directed at a specific individual, its content was chilling.

What do you do?

Suggested Reading: Maulding Green, W., and Leonard, E. (2019). *The Soft Skills of Leadership: Navigating with Confidence and Humility*, 2nd ed., Chapter 3. Lanham, MD: Rowman & Littlefield.

Additional Selected Readings: "To Be a Great Leader, You Have to Learn How to Delegate Well." *Harvard Business Review Digital Articles*, 2–6.

CHRISTMAS CHEER?

The safety and security of students is uppermost in the mind of every campus leader. In the case of child custody situations, it is important to know the law in order to make correct decisions.

On a Friday afternoon in December approximately an hour and a half before scheduled dismissal for the Christmas holidays, a noncustodial parent arrives at school to pick up his son. The secretary, knowing that the father does not have legal custody, refuses his request. He immediately becomes angry and tries to bully the secretary to get his son. The father says he is taking his child out of the country for Christmas; if he waits until school is dismissed, they will miss their flight; the entire holiday will be ruined and threatens that the principal "will pay." He further threatens to "have the principal's job," "have her arrested," and other remarks in an attempt to intimidate her.

What action would you take?

____

____

____

____

____

____

____

Suggested Reading: Maulding Green, W., and Leonard, E. (2019). *The Soft Skills of Leadership: Navigating with Confidence and Humility*, 2nd ed., Chapter 3. Lanham, MD: Rowman & Littlefield.

Additional Selected Reading: Williams, J., and Lebsock, S. (2018). "Now What?" Retrieved from https://hbr.org/cover-story/2018/01/now-what.

SAFETY FIRST

Monday morning, a parent comes into your office to inform you that on Friday a student in her daughter's class had threatened to kill all the students in class. The student proclaimed that he was psychotic, had a "blade," and was going to use it. Moreover, the student stated that his mother was going to beat the teacher to a pulp. The classmate further told her mother that this student always talks about "voices in his head talking to him."

What do you do?

____

____

____

____

____

____

____

Suggested Reading: Maulding Green, W., and Leonard, E. (2019). *The Soft Skills of Leadership: Navigating with Confidence and Humility*, 2nd ed., Chapter 3. Lanham, MD: Rowman & Littlefield.

Additional Selected Reading: Lin, Xialing, Spence, P. R., and Lachlan, K. A. (2016). "Social Media and Credibility Indicators: The Effect of Influence Cues." *Computers in Human Behavior*, *63*, 264–71.

2

CONTRIBUTING AUTHOR'S OPTIONS FOR CREDIBILITY SJTS

SO MANY PROBLEMS, SO LITTLE TIME

A. Get to the ballgame as quickly as you can; the parent knows you are busy.
B. Relegate the issue to an assistant principal and hope they follow-up.
C. Fulfill the commitment you made to the parent and take the time to call.
D. Wait till Monday to investigate the issue; it's Friday and you have a pep rally!
E. Another option:

____

____

____

SEARCHING FOR ANSWERS

A. Notify student's parents, and send him home for a day.
B. Expel the student from school.
C. Suspend student for three days.
D. Place student in *In-School Suspension*.
E. Thank the student for his honesty, warn him about the dangers of drugs, and have him return to class.
F. Contact the police and the parents of the student.
G. Another option:

____

____

____

PRINCIPLE I: SIMPLICITY

A. Suspend the child, and copy and paste the notes as you were told.
B. Suspend the child, and do not include the counseling notes.
C. Meet with the parents, and do not suspend the child.
D. Wait out the situation, and let the principal handle it when she returns.
E. Another option:

____

____

____

THE DIGITAL AGE

A. Since the post is on the student's personal Facebook site and police are aware, just make a note of the incident.
B. Discuss with the police any action that should be taken.
C. Contact and meet with the parents to discuss the incident.
D. Consult with mental health professionals.
E. Suspend student from school for five days.
F. Student cannot return to school without a psychiatrist's confirmation that he is not a risk to others.
G. Note the incident and ask parents to notify you if there are any other issues.
H. Another option:

____

____

____

CHRISTMAS CHEER?

A. Contact the custodial parent to get permission to release the child early.
B. Review the parents' divorce decree to confirm the father's legal status regarding his child and keep the child in school until the end of the day.
C. Notify the district office of the situation.
D. Call the campus school resource officer (SRO) to have the father arrested for his threats and disruptive behavior.
E. Another option:

____

____

____

SAFETY FIRST

A. Interview the female student to determine what happened in class.
B. Contact the parents of the student making the threats.
C. This parent has been a troublemaker and the teacher never mentioned it. Just make a note of the incident.
D. Contact the police to find out what to do.
E. Interview the teacher about the incident.
F. Suspend the student pending investigation.
G. Consult mental health professionals.
H. Immediately remove the student from class. Search for weapons.
I. Student not allowed back in school without a psychiatrist's confirmation that student is not a risk to others.
J. Expel student from school.
K. Another option:

____
____
____

3

LESSONS ON COMPETENCE

Professional competence requires constant renewal. K–12 education leaders, whether at the elementary, middle school, or high school levels. Some rise through the ranks in K–12 education while a few, where allowed in some states, join the ranks of K–12 education leaders from areas outside K–12 education. Regardless of the path to leadership, these individuals must master their trade and doing so requires constant renewal and an unwavering devotion to lifelong learning. The credo of K–12 education leaders, like that of leaders in all areas, should be that they will remain current and thoroughly knowledgeable in their field. That they will be competent in their chosen field.

The scenarios in this chapter are, in one way or another, related to a leader's Competence. If your Leader Acumen assessment scores indicated this as an area for needed growth, you should work through the scenarios with a couple of things in mind. First, as you work through the scenarios in the chapter, take particular note of the *Contributing Authors' Options* to each problem at the end of each chapter of SJTs. In working through the scenarios and reviewing the *Contributing Authors' Options*, one of the two things will happen. You will find disparity between your responses and the authors, or you might, indeed, find that your responses coincide with the authors' (see Appendix B for a graphic representation). Next, reflect on the information you gained from the LEA assessment. If you acknowledge that Competence is an area for growth based on the assessment, ask yourself if this was based on your Self assessment, the Circle assessment, or both.

If either or both assessments (the Self or Circle) indicate that you have room for improvement in the area of leader Competence *and* you are also finding disparity in yours and the *Contributing Authors' Options*, chances are you will find growth via working through these exercises and accompanying readings. However, be reminded, this will not happen overnight. Growing your *Leader Acumen* is a worthy endeavor but is a painstakingly time-consuming undertaking. It requires rewiring of your thought processes regarding learnings that are very ingrained into your most innate understandings and this takes time (see Appendix B for a graphic representation).

On the other hand, if you find your solutions and the solutions offered in the *Contributing Authors' Options* coincide highly, yet your Self score is lower than the mean shown at the end of your Leader Acumen assessment for Competence, one of the two things is happening. Either you are lacking in self-confidence, yet your decision-making is solid; or conversely, perhaps you are somewhat overconfident but nonetheless making good decisions. If the first is the case, working through the scenarios should enhance your self-confidence. The second option (overconfidence) is the one to be most wary of. Leaders in this category many times find themselves derailed as leaders, even though they generally are good decision makers. Working through the scenarios should help to instill the idea that there is more than one acceptable solution to most problems/issues and thus lessen one potential major consequence of overconfidence, feeling that you have the only viable solution.

If you opt to have a Circle/360 assessment done and find that your solutions and the solutions offered in the *Contributing Authors' Options* coincide highly, yet your Circle scores were outside the standard deviation (available from the LEAD team when a Circle/360 assessment is done) for Competence, it is possible that a different set of problems is occurring. Either you are selecting the course of action you believe is best for the scenario, yet in reality you would not implement it, or the problem may be one of *perception*. It is much more likely that it is the former. Only in rare instances would the latter be the case. However, we insert it here for thought because, on occasion, it is the case. And, as the old saying goes, "Perception is reality."

Perhaps you are indeed highly competent yet *perception* is the issue for your low scores in Competence. This could be a case of projection. For example, you may not "look" credible and perhaps for legitimate reasons. You will recall from the chapter on credibility in *The Soft Skills of Leadership: Navigating with Confidence and Humility*, mention was made of how "what you wear" infers or projects an image. Such could be the case in this instance.

Finally, improving your leader acumen and "adaptive capacity" as stated in the preface is a process. As you will recall, the notion of leader acumen is predicated on the theory that there is a genetic predisposition toward leadership.

As Marquis and Tilcsik[1] so aptly noted, imprinting may take place, during brief sensitive periods of high susceptibility during the formative process, during the teachable moment, or another yet different time of susceptibility; and that imprints once established are persistent.

The lessons in this book are to be utilized to grow Leader Acumen in this third way—over the long, repetitive process. To that end and to truly be imprinted with any of the competencies, actions for building the various skill sets may be found in Appendix C.

Again, quoting *The Soft Skills of Leadership: Navigating with Competence and Humility* (2nd edition), "True competence in effectively applying 'hard skills' requires mastery of 'soft skills'—that is, people-centered skills."[2]

CHANGING SCHOOL DYNAMICS

You are the new principal of an elementary school that has seen a significant increase in Hispanic students who are either non-English or very limited English speaking. The veteran teachers of the school have dealt with this as best they can; however, the new teachers are totally frustrated. In order to lower the frustration level of the teachers and ensure students are provided with appropriate language assistance services, what action would you take?

Suggested Reading: Maulding Green, W., and Leonard, E. (2019). *The Soft Skills of Leadership: Navigating with Confidence and Humility*, 2nd ed., Chapter 4. Lanham, MD: Rowman & Littlefield.

Additional Selected Reading: Haynes, Kyle. 2017. "Diversionary Conflict: Demonizing Enemies or Demonstrating Competence?" *Conflict Management and Peace Science 34(4):* 337–58. doi:http://journals.sagepub.com.lynx.lib.usm.edu/loi/cmpb.

TO SERVE OR NOT TO SERVE

Kevin has been diagnosed with attention-deficit hyperactivity disorder (ADHD) over the summer by a psychometrist outside of the school district. This psychometrist states that Kevin is 504 eligible and lists required accommodations to be followed by the school in her report. The student has been given medication for his ADHD. Since the student has been taking the medication, his grades have been in the A to C range with no discipline referrals. A meeting has been scheduled with the parents to discuss the proposed 504 plan.

How do you handle this situation?

____

____

____

____

____

____

____

Suggested Reading: Maulding Green, W., and Leonard, E. (2019). *The Soft Skills of Leadership: Navigating with Confidence and Humility*, 2nd ed., Chapter 4. Lanham, MD: Rowman & Littlefield.

Additional Selected Readings: Burton, D., South, G., Pickering, A., and Start, A. (2016). "Emotional and Motivational Correlates of Leadership Styles: A Comprehensive Framework for Understanding Effective Leaders." *Journal of Leadership Studies*, *10*(3), 22–40. doi:10.1002/jls.21485.

TO ERR IS HUMAN

You are a new principal taking over a very successful school for your first job as a building principal. The school has a strong academic tradition and has done well on state assessments in the past. During your first year, the state has implemented a new evaluation system that all teachers must participate in during the school year. The school year has been pretty smooth but one major transition has been an increase in accountability especially with professional responsibilities and making sure all decisions are student-focused.

One particular teacher has been really nervous about the new evaluation process. The teacher is a special education math teacher who does some inclusion and learning strategies classes. The teacher has had a decent year, but some minor changes have been requested during drop-in visits. During one of her formal observations, she worked several math problems wrong. The students seem confused and unsure of what to do next.

If you are the administrator conducting the observation, what actions would you take to address the situation?

Suggested Reading: Maulding Green, W., and Leonard, E. (2019). *The Soft Skills of Leadership: Navigating with Confidence and Humility*, 2nd ed., Chapter 4. Lanham, MD: Rowman & Littlefield.

Additional Selected Reading: Crocker, A., Gardner, H. K., and Cross, R. (2018). "How to Make Sure Agile Teams Can Work Together." *Harvard Business School Cases*, 1.

MEET THE PRESS

A parent comes in to report a bullying situation is taking place at school and on the bus. Nothing has been reported to the counselors or school administrators. After investigation, it appears that the interactions (bullying) have been taking place in the neighborhood. Nonetheless, a plan was put in place to report any school-related problems to an administrator, and the parents were assured that any school-related incidents would be addressed.

Sometime thereafter, there was a short exchange of words (name-calling) on one occasion in the hallway between classes. The name-caller received school discipline as indicated by policy, and the parents of the name-caller were contacted. Several weeks pass and the reporting parent comes back demanding to know what had been done to deal with the name-caller. During the conference, it was obvious that the parent was "under the influence." The parent vacillated between hostility and falling asleep (at which time her daughter would kick her foot to wake her up). We explained that nothing other than the one incident had taken place at school or on the bus and that actions had been taken to address that particular situation. The parent demanded to know the specific actions currently being taken.

Later, the parent went to the local news station to complaint. The news station interviewed the child and did a full story regarding the bullying that was being allowed at school. Two weeks later, another local television station shows up to film and interview additional students as they leave campus.

The same parent also enters the building and attempts to check out students other than her daughter to be interviewed by the reporter. She is asked to leave campus and refuses.

1. How do you handle the news reporter?

2. How do you handle the parent?

Suggested Reading: Maulding Green, W., and Leonard, E. (2019). *The Soft Skills of Leadership: Navigating with Confidence and Humility*, 2nd ed., Chapter 4. Lanham, MD: Rowman & Littlefield.

Additional Selected Reading: Sadun, Raffaella, Bloom, Nicholas, and Reenen, John V. (2017). "Why Do We Undervalue Competent Management? Neither Great Leadership nor Brilliant Strategy Matters without Operational Excellence." *Harvard Business Review*, *95*(5), 120–27.

IT'S LONELY AT THE TOP

One of the things I did not realize when I became a superintendent was that no one calls you and tells you, "Hey, it's really poor weather today and the kids should not go to school." Typically, this decision is made solely by the superintendent—especially in smaller rural districts. You have to develop a system of checks and measures (e.g., a certain bridge for ice, etc.) that you monitor when the weather threatens to make travel treacherous for students and staff. Sure, you will get input from the local weather services, which you should build a relationship with early on. But, ultimately the decision rests with you.

The current situation is you are in the midst of one of the coldest weather patterns in your area in decades. You are already on your fifth snow day, and some of the other districts in your region are able to run their buses due to melting that occurs in their areas but not yours. As a first-year superintendent, you feel the pressure mounting to try for your kids and staff to go to school, as there have not been this many snow days in one year in decades.

What do you do?

Suggested Reading: Maulding Green, W., and Leonard, E. (2019). *The Soft Skills of Leadership: Navigating with Confidence and Humility*, 2nd ed., Chapter 4. Lanham, MD: Rowman & Littlefield.

Additional Selected Reading: Vidic, Z., Burton, D., South, G., Pickering, A., and Start, A. (2016). "Emotional and Motivational Correlates of Leadership Styles: A Comprehensive Framework for Understanding Effective Leaders." *Journal of Leadership Studies*, *10*(3), 22–40. doi:10.1002/jls.21485.

LITTLE MISS SUNSHINE

You receive a note written by a parent that states, "Please put my daughter on a seat on the bus where the sun doesn't shine on her. She gets hot on the ride home each day, sweats, and the bus has no air conditioning!"

How do you respond?

____

____

____

____

____

____

____

Suggested Reading: Maulding Green, W., and Leonard, E. (2019). *The Soft Skills of Leadership: Navigating with Confidence and Humility*, 2nd ed., Chapter 4. Lanham, MD: Rowman & Littlefield.

Additional Selected Reading: Pihlainen, V., Kivinen, T., and Lammintakanen, J. (2016). "Management and Leadership Competence in Hospitals: A Systematic Literature Review." *Leadership in Health Services (1751–1879)*, *29*(1), 95–110. doi:10.1108/LHS-11-2014-0072.

CHARMIN SOFT?

Your custodian tells you that the toilet in the third-grade boy's restroom keeps getting clogged. She notices a child bringing a box of baby wipes with him to the bathroom several times a day and suspects that the baby wipes are clogging the toilet. You call the school system's plumber who inspects the toilet and confirms the toilet is clogged with baby wipes. You e-mail the teachers asking the teachers not to allow students to bring baby wipes to the restrooms. The next day, you receive a phone call from a parent who is complaining that her child is not allowed to bring his baby wipes to the restroom. She further explains that her child, a special education student, is not good at wiping with toilet paper, has an aversion to toilet paper, and the baby wipes are more suitable for his needs.

How do you respond to the third grader's parent?

Suggested Reading: Maulding Green, W., and Leonard, E. (2019). *The Soft Skills of Leadership: Navigating with Confidence and Humility*, 2nd ed., Chapter 4. Lanham, MD: Rowman & Littlefield.

Additional Selected Reading: Giles, Sunnie. (2016). "The Most Important Leadership Competencies, According to Leaders Around the World." Retrieved from https://hbr.org/2016/03/the-most-important-leadership-competencies-according-to-leaders-around-the-world.

UNABLE TO WALK THE LINE

You are the principal of a high school. One of your teachers was reported as having odd behavior during carline/bus dismissal duty. When he was approached by another teacher and asked if something was wrong, the teacher became defensive. Before he made it back to his classroom, a half-empty bottle of whisky was found in his classroom by the janitor.

What should you do?

____

____

____

____

____

____

____

Suggested Reading: Maulding Green, W., and Leonard, E. (2019). *The Soft Skills of Leadership: Navigating with Confidence and Humility*, 2nd ed., Chapter 4. Lanham, MD: Rowman & Littlefield.

Additional Selected Readings: O'Hara, C. (2018). "How to Manage an Employee Who's Having a Personal Crisis." *Harvard Business Review Digital Articles*, 2–6.

BLOODY MESS—PART I

Your school's cafeteria manager has come to you to complain about one of the cafeteria workers. The manager states that the worker is no longer remembering how to cook basic foods that she has cooked for years. She is concerned that the employee is showing signs of dementia. You agree to speak with the worker after the lunch waves. In the meantime, you call human resources (HR) for assistance and share the manager's concerns. A few minutes later, you receive a text message from one of the teachers with a picture of bloody piece of chicken on a child's plate. You rush to the cafeteria to see what is going on. When you arrive, you realize that many of the children are biting into bloody chicken.

PUT THE STEPS LISTED BELOW IN THE ORDER YOU THINK THEY SHOULD OCCUR

A. Have the manager check the temperature of the bloody chicken served.
B. Instruct the manager to keep a piece of the bloody chicken in case children get sick and the chicken needs to be tested.
C. Call HR again to see what they recommend to be done.
D. Contact the parents of the children who had bloody chicken to let them know to circumvent rumors.
E. Give the students who had bloody chicken a new lunch plate.
F. Thank the teacher who let you know about the problem.
G. Privately, orally reprimand the manager and worker for not checking the temperature of the chicken.

____

____

____

____

____

____

____

Suggested Reading: Maulding Green, W., and Leonard, E. (2019). *The Soft Skills of Leadership: Navigating with Confidence and Humility*, 2nd ed., Chapter 4. Lanham, MD: Rowman & Littlefield.

Additional Selected Reading: Gukdo, B., Ye, D., Soojin, L., and Seungwan, K. (2017). "Leader Trust, Competence, LMX, and Member Performance: A Moderated Mediation Framework." *Psychological Reports*, *120*(6), 1137–59. doi:10.1177/0033294117716465.

BLOODY MESS—PART II

Once the lunch waves are over, you meet again with the cafeteria manager to determine how bloody chicken was served to the students. The manager claims the cafeteria worker she was concerned about forgot to check the temperature of the chicken and forgot to record that temperature in the logbook as required.

PUT THE STEPS LISTED BELOW IN THE ORDER YOU THINK THEY SHOULD OCCUR

A. Meet with the cafeteria worker to get her side of the story and ask her if she has dementia.
B. Inform HR and the superintendent of your actions to correct the situation.
C. Act on the advice of HR to, along with the manager, meet with the worker and document the situation to see if it becomes a pattern.
D. Privately, orally reprimand the manager for not checking the temperature of the chicken.
E. Ask the cafeteria worker if she has dementia.
F. Have the manager, privately, orally reprimand the worker for not checking the temperature of the chicken.

Suggested Reading: Maulding Green, W., and Leonard, E. (2019). *The Soft Skills of Leadership: Navigating with Confidence and Humility*, 2nd ed., Chapter 4. Lanham, MD: Rowman & Littlefield.

Additional Selected Reading: Portnova, I., and Peiseniece, L. (2017). "Leaders' Competences for Successful Leadership of Invention and Implementation of Innovation: A Conceptual Model." *Journal of Business Management*, *13*, 40–55.

4

CONTRIBUTING AUTHORS' OPTIONS FOR COMPETENCE SJTS

CHANGING SCHOOL DYNAMICS

A. Suggest that the teachers research effective strategies during their planning period.
B. Provide no support since these are "trained" teachers.
C. Provide PD by showing videos for teachers to watch on EL strategies during a faculty meeting. Additionally, provide a "Make It and Take It" workshop to make labels for the school designed to help the Hispanic students learn the English words for school items such as door, window, table, chair, and so forth.
D. Provide guided PD with feedback to include strategies, language development, and cultural dynamics.
E. Provide a program such as Duolingo to enable teachers to speak to their students in their native language.
F. Another option:

____

____

____

TO SERVE OR NOT TO SERVE

A. Give the psychometrist's report to the teacher to follow the recommendations listed.
B. Provide information on ADHD so that the teacher will understand the disorder and can provide accommodations.

C. Have the students in his class provide peer support to help Kevin keep up with his school work and assignments.
D. Tell the parents that the school will not follow the accommodations by an outside psychometrist.
E. Although the school is not required to follow the psychometrist's diagnosis and recommendations, the report will initiate a discussion of the student's performance and determine the next steps. The process for the next steps will be discussed.
F. Another option:

___

___

___

TO ERR IS HUMAN

A. You do not say anything.
B. You address the situation after class.
C. You address her in the post-conference meeting.
D. You correct the mistakes in class in a very professional manner making sure you do not embarrass the teacher.
E. Another option:

___

___

___

MEET THE PRESS

A. Leave the reporter alone since she is parked off campus.
B. Ask the reporter to leave.
C. Call the police.
D. Address the reporter and ask what her intentions are so that you can establish guidelines.
E. Another option:

___

___

___

MEET THE PRESS/QUESTION 2

A. Let her check the students out and talk to them at the end of school.
B. Explain to her that she cannot talk to other students and that she must leave campus.

C. Call the police and have her escorted off campus.
D. Tell her she must wait until school is over to talk to students.
E. Another option:

____

____

____

IT'S LONELY AT THE TOP

A. You try it the next day because some of the other districts are. You have got to get the kids back in school to prepare them for the state test.
B. You put the safety of your students and staff first. Err on the side of caution and wait for the roads to clear.
C. Regardless of the conditions, you make the statement that we will go to school in two days regardless of what the weather looks like. We have to prepare our kids.
D. You delegate the decision to the transportation director who has been with the district for a decade and who knows the routes the buses travel and the potential problem areas well.
E. Another option:

____

____

____

LITTLE MISS SUNSHINE

A. Ignore the request.
B. Check with the school nurse to see if the child has a medical issue.
C. Give the note to the bus driver to handle.
D. Contact the parent and ask if they have a special seat in their car for their child that prevents the sun from shining on her.
E. Another option:

____

____

____

CHARMIN SOFT?

A. Allow the child to keep bringing baby wipes as long as he throws them away in the trash can.

B. Tell the parent the baby wipes are clogging the toilets.
C. Check to see if baby wipe usage is in the child's IEP.
D. Ask the parent to purchase biodegradable/flushable baby wipes that can be flushed.
E. Another option:

____

____

____

UNABLE TO WALK THE LINE

A. Call the local authorities or school police force and have them give the teacher a sobriety test.
B. Have the teacher report to the principal's office and confront him.
C. Block his car in so that he can't leave, and then call the police.
D. Another option:

____

____

____

Bloody Mess—Part I
No Options Needed
Bloody Mess—Part II
No Options Needed

5

LESSONS ON ABILITY TO INSPIRE

When our intent as a leader is to inspire, we often fall short of our goal. For some reason, as leaders, we believe that inspiration is some mystical/magical force that only coaches and motivational speakers possess. Although inspiration can sometimes include the elements of high energy and mountain-moving motivation, inspiration is best achieved through what we do and say.

The scenarios in this chapter are, in one way or another, related to a leader's Ability to Inspire. If your LEA assessment scores indicated this as an area for needed growth, you should work through the scenarios with a couple of things in mind. First, as you work through the scenarios in the chapter take particular note of the *Contributing Authors' Options* to each problem at the end of each chapter of SJTs. In working through the scenarios and reviewing the *Contributing Authors' Options*, one of the two things will happen. You will find disparity between your responses and the authors, or you might, indeed, find that your responses coincide with the authors' (see Appendix B for a graphic representation). Next, reflect on the information you gained from the Leader Acumen assessment. If you acknowledge that Ability to Inspire is an area for growth based on the assessment, ask yourself if this was based on your Self assessment, the Circle assessment, or both.

If either or both assessments (the Self or Circle) indicate that you have room for improvement in the area of leader Ability to Inspire *and* you are also finding disparity in yours and the *Contributing Authors' Options*, chances are you will find growth via working through these exercises and accompanying readings. However, be reminded, this will not happen overnight. Growing your *Leader Acumen* is a worthy endeavor but is a painstakingly time-consuming undertaking. It requires rewiring of your thought processes regarding learnings that are very ingrained into your most innate understandings and this takes time (see Appendix B for a graphic representation).

On the other hand, if you find that your solutions and the solutions offered in the *Contributing Authors' Options* coincide highly, yet your Self score is lower than the mean shown at the end of your Leader Acumen assessment for Ability to Inspire, one of the two things is happening. Either you are lacking in self-confidence, yet your decision-making is solid; or conversely, perhaps you are somewhat overconfident but nonetheless making good decisions. If the first is the case, working through the scenarios should enhance your self-confidence. The second option (overconfidence) is the one to be most wary of. Leaders in this category many times find themselves derailed as leaders, even though they generally are good decision makers. Working through the scenarios should help to instill the idea that there is more than one acceptable solution to most problems/issues and thus lessen one potential major consequence of overconfidence, feeling that you have the only viable solution.

If you opt to have a Circle/360 assessment done and find that your solutions and the solutions offered in the *Contributing Authors' Options* coincide highly, yet your Circle scores were outside the standard deviation (available from the LEAD team when a Circle/360 assessment is done) for Ability to Inspire, it is possible that a different set of problems is occurring. Either you are selecting the course of action you believe is best for the scenario, yet in reality you would not implement it, or the problem may be one of *perception*. It is much more likely that it is the former. Only in rare instances would the latter be the case. However, we insert it here for thought because, on occasion, it is the case. And, as the old saying goes, "Perception is reality."

Perhaps you are indeed highly inspirational, yet *perception* is the issue for your low scores in Ability to Inspire. This could be a case of projection. For example, you may not "look" inspirational and perhaps for legitimate reasons. You will recall from the chapter on credibility in *The Soft Skills of Leadership: Navigating with Confidence and Humility*, mention was made of how "what you wear" infers or projects an image. Such could be the case in this instance.

Finally, improving your leader acumen and "adaptive capacity" as stated in the preface is a process. As you will recall, the notion of leader acumen is predicated on the theory that there is a genetic predisposition toward leadership.

As Marquis and Tilcsik[1] so aptly noted, imprinting may take place, during brief sensitive periods of high susceptibility during the formative process, during the teachable moment, or another yet different time of susceptibility; and that imprints once established are persistent. The lessons in this book are to be utilized to grow Leader Acumen in this third way—over the long, repetitive process. To that end and to truly be imprinted with any of the competencies, actions for building the various skill sets may be found in Appendix C.

> True inspiration for both the leader and peers and followers comes from within by finding value and meaning in the work they do.[2]

CRUNCH TIME

School finance is at the forefront of conversations among school leaders now more than ever. With the increased pressure of accountability results on schools and districts, superintendents and principals are faced with various budget decisions while trying to invest more in academics.

When budget cuts have to be made to adjust for a decrease in local or state funds, difficult decisions have to be made. It is even more difficult when cuts are handed down by the state in the middle of the year when contracts for employees have already been awarded and must be honored.

After a statewide economic decline, a budget cut is handed down in the middle of the year requiring all state agencies to reduce their budgets by 5 percent for the remainder of the year. This cut is coupled with a sudden increase in fuel prices causing the district's fuel cost to increase over $1,000 a day. Additionally, the district is experiencing tremendous student growth.

After surviving the first budget dilemma in the midyear, it becomes obvious that additional cuts are looming for the next year. The projected budget for the next school year is at least $4 million less than the previous year.

How do you balance the budget given these variables?

Suggested Reading: Maulding Green, W., and Leonard, E. (2019). *The Soft Skills of Leadership: Navigating with Confidence and Humility*, 2nd ed., Chapter 5. Lanham, MD: Rowman & Littlefield.

Additional Selected Reading: Bawany, S. (2016). "Leadership during Turbulent Times." *Leadership Excellence Essentials*, *33*(12), 18

ONE FOR THE ROAD?

Katie, a kindergarten student, was a sweet, mature, and inquisitive child. Her mom had a history of drug abuse, and the grandparents were actively involved in raising her. One Friday afternoon, no one arrived to pick Katie up. After waiting in the office for about half an hour, her mom arrived. It was apparent she was in an altered state when she entered the front office. As principal, you immediately ask the school receptionist to take Katie down to the snack room for a treat. You invite Katie's mom to have a seat in the front office.

Once Katie was safely out of the immediate area, you ask the parent to walk into your office. You also requested the school bookkeeper to accompany the two of you and serve as a witness to the conversation. You then explain to the parent that you will not allow her to take Katie as you are fairly certain that she is under the influence of drugs and/or alcohol. The parent screams, yells, and basically has a meltdown before storming out of your office. However, in her altered state, she could not remember how to exit the office suite and ends up back in your office a few minutes later, this time demanding to talk to someone about picking up her child.

You once again explain your decision. The mother is in such a state that she does not realize she is speaking to the same person, in the same office that she had spoken to earlier. This obviously speaks clearly to the level of her altered state!

What should be done next?

____

____

____

____

____

____

____

Suggested Reading: Maulding Green, W., and Leonard, E. (2019). *The Soft Skills of Leadership: Navigating with Confidence and Humility*, 2nd ed., Chapter 5. Lanham, MD: Rowman & Littlefield.

Additional Selected Reading: Jiang, J., Gao, A., and Yang, B. (2018). "Employees' Critical Thinking, Leaders' Inspirational Motivation, and Voice Behavior: The Mediating Role of Voice Efficacy." *Journal of Personnel Psychology*, *17*(1), 33–41. doi:10.1027/1866-5888/a000193.

KEEPING YOUR PROMISE

The Building Leadership Team (BLT) had made big plans during the summer planning meeting to celebrate academic achievement, attendance, and behavior by rewarding students with a field day during the last month of school. Students achieved the established goals and received monthly recognition leading up to the grand finale—Field Day. Three weeks prior to the big day, you receive an emergency phone call that requires your immediate attention and will require your absence for the remainder of the school year. You agree to move forward with Field Day, keeping your promise to recognize student achievement. A big fight occurs during the event that warrants serious disciplinary actions against several students. Law enforcement gets involved and Emergency Medical Services (EMS) is needed to handle injured students. You are responsible since you authorized this event. The assistant superintendent wants an immediate resolution upon your return to school due to extensive media coverage of this situation. School is out for the summer.

What do you do?

Suggested Reading: Maulding Green, W., and Leonard, E. (2019). *The Soft Skills of Leadership: Navigating with Confidence and Humility*, 2nd ed., Chapter 5. Lanham, MD: Rowman & Littlefield.

Additional Selected Reading: Goleman, D., and Boyatzis, R. E. (2017). "Emotional Intelligence Has 12 Elements. Which Do You Need to Work On?" *Harvard Business Review Digital Articles*, 2–5.

DOMESTIC VIOLENCE—PART I

The doorbell at your home rings in the middle of the night. You open it to find one of your best teachers screaming for help. She has her children with her and is in a state of panic. You let them in, and she proceeds to tell you that her husband attacked her in front of the children and threatened to kill her. The children are shaken, scared, and visibly upset as is your teacher. The teacher has shared with you some incidences of abuse in the past. Additionally, she has shared with you times she has left her husband but you know the separation usually doesn't last for long before they reconcile. This time, the teacher appears terrified and is in fear of her life.

What steps will you take to help your teacher?

Suggested Reading: Maulding Green, W., and Leonard, E. (2019). *The Soft Skills of Leadership: Navigating with Confidence and Humility*, 2nd ed., Chapter 5. Lanham, MD: Rowman & Littlefield.

Additional Selected Reading: Karp, T. (2013). "Studying Subtle Acts of Leadership." *Leadership*, *9*(1), 3–22.

DOMESTIC VIOLENCE—PART II

The teacher is too scared to show up at school the next day. She takes personal leave to relocating herself and the children. You notice her husband's car driving past your school and in your parking lot. You call the police to make a report and notify the teacher he is on campus. Later that day, you receive an e-mail from a stranger. The stranger claims the husband was giving away his personal and valuable belongings stating he didn't need them anymore because he was homicidal and suicidal. The stranger also states that the husband says he will come into the school and shoot to kill his wife. He (the stranger) is aware the wife isn't on campus that day because the husband told him her vehicle wasn't there.

How will you ensure the safety of your students and faculty given the situation?

____

____

____

____

____

____

____

Suggested Reading: Maulding Green, W., and Leonard, E. (2019). *The Soft Skills of Leadership: Navigating with Confidence and Humility*, 2nd ed., Chapter 5. Lanham, MD: Rowman & Littlefield.

Additional Selected Reading: Meyerson, D. E. (2001). "Radical Change, the Quiet Way." *Harvard Business Review*, *79*(9), 92–100.

POPULAR REQUEST OF A DIFFERENT KIND

During "Meet the Teacher" day (before school begins), your office is flooded with parents demanding you remove their children from a specific teacher's classroom. Parents claim they are uncomfortable with their child in this class, and some even accuse you of not liking them or their child because you've put their child in this teacher's class. You've not had any problems with the teacher in years past, nor has this teacher gotten poor evaluations from you. Interestingly, you have noticed that this teacher has a bad habit of closing her eyes for an extended period of time when she speaks to you and to other adults. It's awkward to hold conversations with her because of this, but you don't see her display this habit with the students. She fully engages with kids and keeps her eyes open when conversing and teaching.

How do you respond to the parents and handle this situation?

____

____

____

____

____

____

____

Suggested Reading: Maulding Green, W., and Leonard, E. (2019). *The Soft Skills of Leadership: Navigating with Confidence and Humility*, 2nd ed., Chapter 5. Lanham, MD: Rowman & Littlefield.

Additional Selected Reading: Nayar, Vineet. (2013). "Three Differences between Managers and Leaders." Retrieved from https://hbr.org/2013/08/tests-of-a-leadership-transiti.

A PROM DILEMMA

During the weeks leading up to the Junior–Senior Prom, the voting process starts to name the Prom King and Queen. Among the list of names submitted for the Prom King is John Smith. John Smith is actually Joanna Smith. Joanna is a female student who identifies as a male. John/Joanna's parents support their child's decision and have officially changed their child's name to "John" in the school records. John/Joanna's parents engaged an attorney, and after a preliminary hearing the school district's attorney says to treat John/Joanna as a male student.

As the election date draws near for the Prom vote, it is clearly evident that John/Joanna holds an overwhelming margin of student support for Prom King. The parents of other Prom King candidates are calling the school asking for appointments with the principal, assistant principals, the senior class sponsor, or anyone else who will listen to their complaint. The complaint is simple: how can the administrators allow this to occur?

To complicate the matter even more, the top five contenders for Prom Queen have all joined together and have written a letter to the principal and provided a statement outlining their refusal to have the customary "First Dance" with a girl dressed as a boy. The letter is signed by each girl and states that such a dance is against the moral convictions of each girl.

The election is three days away.

As an administrator, how do you work to resolve these issues and let the students enjoy their Junior–Senior Prom?

____

____

____

____

____

____

____

Suggested Reading: Maulding Green, W., and Leonard, E. (2019). *The Soft Skills of Leadership: Navigating with Confidence and Humility*, 2nd ed., Chapter 5. Lanham, MD: Rowman & Littlefield.

Additional Selected Reading: Maner, J. (2016). "Good Bosses Switch between Two Leadership Styles." *Harvard Business Review Digital Articles*, 2–5.

6

CONTRIBUTING AUTHORS' OPTIONS FOR ABILITY TO INSPIRE SJTS

CRUNCH TIME

A. Reduce staff across the district. With a growing population, this would certainly increase class sizes by five to six per class.
B. Use reserve funds that are there for emergencies (like a 5 percent cut in the middle of the year) and for future growth of the facilities across the district. This would be a one-time fix as the emergency funds would not be there for the next budget. Ed what about this wording? Ok??
C. Reduce salaries of all employees in the district in order to meet the required cut and maintain the current number of teachers and support personnel.
D. Ask for an increase in local taxes to the limit allowed by law and combine that tax increase with a freeze on hiring, travel, and other modifiable expenses.
E. Another option:

____

____

____

ONE FOR THE ROAD?

A. Call the school resource officer for assistance. Intoxicated people are unpredictable.
B. Call the local child welfare agency for assistance. Releasing the child to the intoxicated mother could be dangerous for the child.
C. Call the resource officer and the child welfare agency as action by both may be needed.

D. Call the superintendent to inform her of the situation and to ask for advice while the resource officer is on the way.
E. Another option:

____

____

____

KEEPING YOUR PROMISE

A. Refer to law enforcement for further investigation and press charges against students.
B. Go on vacation and deal with it later.
C. Immediately suspend all students involved, pending expulsion.
D. Direct your assistant principal to handle the matter.
E. Conduct a full investigation upon your return, and then take appropriate disciplinary action.
F. Another option:

____

____

____

DOMESTIC VIOLENCE—PART I

A. Call the police and support her as she files a police report.
B. Offer to let the teacher stay the night at your home.
C. Contact her husband and let him know his family is safe.
D. Call a shelter for abused women and seek immediate help for your teacher.
E. Another option:

____

____

____

DOMESTIC VIOLENCE—PART II

A. Keep school on lockdown until the situation is resolved.
B. Call teacher and tell her to stay home.
C. Call the police and school system resource officer.
D. Hire extra security to stay on campus and protect the teacher and students.

E. Another option:

____

____

____

POPULAR REQUEST OF A DIFFERENT KIND

A. Tell the parents you are not changing their child's homeroom teacher.
B. Meet with each parent individually asking for specific reasons for the request moving students.
C. Meet with the teacher to discuss how her bad habit is causing problems with first impressions and scheduling.
D. Change all of the schedules.
E. Another option:

____

____

____

A PROM DILEMMA

A. Tell the Prom Queen contenders if they feel they need to refuse to dance with the duly elected Prom King due to moral convictions, then they should remove their respective names from the Prom Queen ballot.
B. Call John to the office and explain to him if he was a real man he would accept the fact that he is a girl.
C. For the sake of transparency, invite the parents of all the students nominated for Prom King and Prom Queen to the school and allow them to conduct the election, count the votes, and declare the winners based on their vote counts.
D. Let the election run its course. If the elected Prom Queen refuses to dance with the elected Prom King for the traditional "First Dance," then continue the evening without a "First Dance."
E. Another option:

____

____

____

7

LESSONS ON VISION

In *The Soft Skills of Leadership: Navigating with Confidence and Humility*, the authors share that "vision as defined in the Leader Acumen model is the end result of a process whereby a leader develops objectives or goals and sets a direction for an organization based on the shared input of all stakeholders. Defining vision is simple. Creating a shared vision and, more significantly, effectively communicating that shared vision, and transforming it into action is the challenge."[1]

The scenarios in this chapter are in one way or another, related to a leader's Vision. If your Leader Acumen assessment scores indicated this as an area for needed growth, you should work through the scenarios with a couple of things in mind. First, as you work through the scenarios in the chapter take particular note of the *Contributing Authors' Options* to each problem at the end of each chapter of SJTs. In working through the scenarios and reviewing the *Contributing Authors' Options*, one of the two things will happen. You will find disparity between your responses and the authors, or you might, indeed, find that your responses coincide with the authors' (see Appendix B for a graphic representation). Next, reflect on the information you gained from the Leader Acumen assessment. If you acknowledge that Vision is an area for growth based on the assessment, ask yourself if this was based on your Self assessment, the Circle assessment, or both.

If either or both assessments (the Self or Circle) indicate that you have room for improvement in the area of leader Vision *and* you are also finding disparity in yours and the *Contributing Authors' Options*, chances are that you will find growth via working through these exercises and accompanying readings. However, be reminded, this will not happen overnight. Growing your *Leader Acumen* is a worthy endeavor but is a painstakingly time-consuming undertaking. It requires rewiring of your thought processes regarding learnings that are very ingrained into your most innate understandings and this takes time (see Appendix B for a graphic representation).

On the other hand, if you find your solutions and the solutions offered in the *Contributing Authors' Options* coincide highly, yet your Self score is lower than the mean shown at the end of your Leader Acumen assessment for Vision, one of the two things is happening. Either you are lacking in self-confidence, yet your decision-making is solid; or conversely, perhaps you are somewhat overconfident but nonetheless making good decisions. If the first is the case, working through the scenarios should enhance your self-confidence. The second option (overconfidence) is the one to be most wary of. Leaders in this category many times find themselves derailed as leaders, even though they generally are good decision makers. Working through the scenarios should help to instill the idea that there is more than one acceptable solution to most problem/issues and thus lessen one potential major consequence of overconfidence, feeling that you have the only viable solution.

If you opt to have a Circle/360 assessment done and find that your solutions and the solutions offered in the *Contributing Authors' Options* coincide highly, yet your Circle scores were outside the standard deviation (available from the LEAD team when a Circle/360 assessment is done) for Vision, it is possible that a different set of problems is occurring. Either you are selecting the course of action you believe is best for the scenario, yet in reality you would not implement it, or the problem may be one of *perception*. It is much more likely that it is the former. Only in rare instances would the latter be the case. However, we insert it here for thought because, on occasion, it is the case. And, as the old saying goes, "Perception is reality."

Perhaps you are indeed highly visionary, yet *perception* is the issue for your low scores in Vision. This could be a case of projection. For example, you may not "look" visionary and perhaps for legitimate reasons. You will recall from the chapter on credibility in *The Soft Skills of Leadership: Navigating with Confidence and Humility*, mention was made of how "what you wear" infers or projects an image. Such could be the case in this instance.

Finally, improving your leader acumen and "adaptive capacity" as stated in the preface is a process. As you will recall, the notion of leader acumen is predicated on the theory that there is a genetic predisposition toward leadership.

As Marquis and Tilcsik[2] so aptly noted, imprinting may take place, during brief sensitive periods of high susceptibility during the formative process, during the teachable moment, or another yet different time of susceptibility; and that imprints once established are persistent.

The lessons in this book are to be utilized to grow Leader Acumen in this third way—over the long, repetitive process. To that end and to truly be imprinted with any of the competencies, actions for building the various skill sets may be found in Appendix C.

> Vision opens the door to opportunities for success for the credible, competent, inspirational leader.[2]

DROPPING AN "F" BOMB

With two weeks left to the end of the year, a student reports to the guidance counselor that their teacher is not teaching and only showing videos on next year's curriculum. Two other students, with discipline issues, report to you that the same teacher has used the "F" word in the classroom.

What do you do?

____

____

____

____

____

____

____

Suggested Reading: Maulding Green, W., and Leonard, E. (2019). *The Soft Skills of Leadership: Navigating with Confidence and Humility*, 2nd ed., Chapter 6. Lanham, MD: Rowman & Littlefield.

Additional Selected Reading: Margolis, J. A., and Ziegert, J. C. (2016). "Vertical Flow of Collectivistic Leadership: An Examination of the Cascade of Visionary Leadership across Levels." *Leadership Quarterly*, *27*(2), 334–48.

SCHOOL IS NEVER BORING

As the leadership team of your school, the principal and assistant must be on the same page and show solidarity when making decisions that could threaten the climate of the school. When the principal is off campus, the assistant principal becomes the administrator in charge. As it happened on the day of the reading fair, you (the principal) are off campus attending a regional administrators' meeting. Community volunteers came in to judge the reading fair and used a rubric to score the reading boards. The winners were selected and announced at the beginning of lunch period, and classes were allowed to view the winning boards leaving the cafeteria. Ribbons had been placed on first, second, third, and honorable mention boards. At the end of the day, an announcement was made that the eighth-grade winners had changed.

The superintendent sends an e-mail to inform you that he needs to meet with you first thing tomorrow morning. The e-mail states that a middle school parent was so upset about a decision concerning her child earlier in the day that she drove forty-five miles to speak with him.

The superintendent meets with you and the assistant principal the next morning to discuss the parental complaint. The parent, Ms. South, stated that her child had initially been awarded first place. However, at the end of the day, her daughter was called to the office and questioned regarding assistance with her project; when the student answered yes, her board was disqualified. The mother wanted to know why her child was the only one called up and questioned. The mother felt that, if called to the office and asked, many of the winning students would say they had had help.

The assistant principal, Mr. North, stated that he was notified at the end of the day that an employee had overheard a teacher say this student had assistance with her board. Mr. North did not have time to conduct a complete investigation.

You are now instructed to complete a full investigation and report findings to the superintendent and then contact the parent. During the ensuing investigation, it is clarified that the child's teacher was teasing the student saying, "I know you didn't do that by yourself." The shy student smiled and did not respond. The employee who overheard part of the conversation did not hear the teacher when she congratulated the student and said good job. The employee went and reported it to the office because the guidelines said students could not have any help.

The superintendent is contacted concerning the findings and advises you to resolve this as soon as possible. He additionally shares that it probably isn't wise to disqualify any more boards at this point.

What should be done?

____

____

____

Suggested Reading: Maulding Green, W., and Leonard, E. (2019). *The Soft Skills of Leadership: Navigating with Confidence and Humility*, 2nd ed., Chapter 6. Lanham, MD: Rowman & Littlefield.

Additional Selected Reading: Anuradha. (2016). "Leadership for the New Age." *Human Capital, 19*(11), 17–9.

INSUBORDINATION?

You call a teacher into your office to discuss her teaching practice and to address a directive you gave all teachers, which she has ignored. The teacher becomes defensive and accusatory, claiming you have ignored her classroom discipline issues. Furthermore, the teacher tells you she will teach the way she has been trained and continue to ignore your directives. The teacher teaches a core course.

What will you do?

Suggested Reading: Maulding Green, W., and Leonard, E. (2019). *The Soft Skills of Leadership: Navigating with Confidence and Humility*, 2nd ed., Chapter 6. Lanham, MD: Rowman & Littlefield.

Additional Selected Reading: Zook, Chris. (2016). "How Dell, HP, and Apple Rediscovered Their Founders' Vision." *Harvard Business Review Digital Articles*, 2–5.

WHERE DO WE GO FROM HERE?

Budget cuts have reduced the number of teachers for the high school where you are principal. As a result, the high school will not be able to offer advanced classes or dual credit in many subjects. Typically, these classes have fewer than ten students because they are only offered to the students with an ACT score of 25 or above and the student must have maintained an "A" average. Due to the pending elimination, a close examination of the criteria needed for dual credit enrollment is implemented. The discovery is made that a student could participate in these classes with an ACT score of 21 or 22 in any of the subtests and with a "C" average in the content area.

What should be done?

____

____

____

____

____

____

____

Suggested Reading: Maulding Green, W., and Leonard, E. (2019). *The Soft Skills of Leadership: Navigating with Confidence and Humility*, 2nd ed., Chapter 6. Lanham, MD: Rowman & Littlefield.

Additional Selected Reading: Watkins, Michael D. (2016). "Leading the Team You Inherit: It's Not the Same as Building One from Scratch." *Harvard Business Review*, (6), 60.

JUST KID'S PLAY?

You are the principal of an elementary school that dismisses before the teacher day is complete. Most of the teachers have children of their own at the school. After students are dismissed, the teachers have forty-five minutes left on the clock. Most days teachers are allowed to plan and work in their rooms; however, once per week, there are faculty meetings. Teacher's kids, for the most part, entertain themselves in their parent's room by doing homework or playing on computers. Some children do go outside and play. Unfortunately, two of the teachers' kids outside playing ended up in a fistfight. This fight resulted in one of the students having to visit the emergency care for stitches. Instead of the teachers coming together to work things out, each took their child's side of the story. One of the teachers called other parents and warned them not to allow their children to play with the child who attacked her child. The child who did the attacking said he was provoked by constant bullying. The mom of this child insists something to be done about the teacher telling parents to stay away from her son. She states this is additional bullying.

What do you do?

____

____

____

____

____

____

____

Suggested Reading: Maulding Green, W., and Leonard, E. (2019). *The Soft Skills of Leadership: Navigating with Confidence and Humility*, 2nd ed., Chapter 6. Lanham, MD: Rowman & Littlefield.

Additional Selected Reading: Nistor, R., and Măluţan, D. (2017). "The Core Values Determine the Effect of Achieving High Performance." *Managerial Challenges of the Contemporary Society*, *10*(2), 80.

ABOUT THAT MOVE

Moving is always a difficult for affected families. Adjusting to new living arrangements impacts all members of the family, especially children who are working to maintain a sense of normalcy and starting over in establishing new friends in new neighborhoods.

Surprisingly, this proposed school move was not a result of a job promotion or moving to another area; the local school district was the driving force behind this move. The school year is coming to an end and the district is proposing to close a school due to a shrinking enrollment caused by an economy that has been steadily declining over the past few years. The district is scrambling for ways to cut costs.

Beverly Mayfield is a community organizer who lives in a quiet and quaint community with very few jobs and low school enrollment. Redistricting students to the neighboring school is the proposed action. Beverly has intentions of contacting news media, filing an OCR complaint, and speaking prior to the school board meeting to voice her opposition to this proposal that she feels is racially motivated.

What do you do?

Suggested Reading: Maulding Green, W., and Leonard, E. (2019). *The Soft Skills of Leadership: Navigating with Confidence and Humility*, 2nd ed., Chapter 6. Lanham, MD: Rowman & Littlefield.

Additional Selected Reading: Rigby, D., Sutherland, J., and Noble, A. (2018). "Agile at Scale." (cover story). *Harvard Business Review, 96*(3), 88–96.

8

CONTRIBUTING AUTHOR'S OPTIONS FOR VISION SJTS

DROPPING AN "F" BOMB

A. Observe the teacher's classroom to see if the allegations are true.
B. Meet with the other teachers to get their opinion of the teacher.
C. Ask parents what they think of the allegations.
D. Meet with the teacher to discuss the allegations.
E. Ignore the remarks as the students who shared them have a major discipline problem.
F. Another option:

____

____

____

SCHOOL IS NEVER BORING

A. Start over and have all of the boards rescored and ask all students if they had help.
B. Apologize to the parent who complained, declare two winners, and award the student who was disqualified a first-place ribbon along with the student who was awarded the blue ribbon when the first student was disqualified.
C. Ask the superintendent for further guidance.
D. Because there was a problem, award each child a certificate of participation, end the reading fair, and move on.

E. Another option:

____

____

____

INSUBORDINATION?

A. You present your view to the teacher and work to reach a compromise.
B. You meet with your leadership team to discuss this teacher.
C. You consult with parents to get advice on this teacher.
D. You let the teacher voice her concerns and let the issue cool off.
E. You charge the teacher with insubordination and dismiss the teacher on the spot.
F. Another option:

____

____

____

WHERE DO WE GO FROM HERE?

A. Scrap the classes.
B. Maintain the criteria and allow only those students to take an online class at the community college (fee is involved, and parents must pay).
C. Allow the students to leave campus to take a class at nearby community college (fee is involved, and parents must pay).
D. Offer the classes every other year.
E. Survey students to determine if changed criteria would create enough interest to fully populate the advanced classes. Survey the teachers to determine if they would be willing to teach an extra prep to keep the advanced classes. Work with the community college to establish a relationship to offer the classes.
F. Another option:

____

____

____

JUST KID'S PLAY?

A. Call teachers in the office together and tell them to work things out.
B. Tell all teachers that they can no longer have their children playing outside.

C. Provide a mandatory daycare after school with supervision on-site at a low cost.
D. Reprimand the teacher for calling parents and discipline the students for fighting on campus.
E. Another option:

____

____

____

ABOUT THAT MOVE

A. Delay the vote until the next school board meeting and hope the issue resolves itself.
B. Vote on the matter, without hearing additional input from Beverly Mayfield.
C. Appoint a task force to further investigate the situation.
D. Inform board members of the situation and proceed as planned.
E. Start from scratch and develop a new plan.
F. Another option:

____

____

____

9

LESSONS ON EMOTIONAL INTELLIGENCE/SOFT SKILLS

Being emotionally intelligent means a lot of things. It includes the ability to recognize emotions in ourselves, controlling or regulating those emotions, acknowledging the same in others, and having a social/relationship awareness. In the last two categories of emotional intelligence (relationship management and social awareness) is where what is currently commonly referred to as "soft skills" falls. Additionally, with the incredible influx of technology into our lives, many of us are not nearly as "in tune" with others as in the past.

It is *critical*, now more than ever in our rapidly advancing, fast-paced society that we give top priority to this crucial relationship building and sustaining skill. In regard to emotional intelligence and the subsequent soft skills therein, we must ask—does the leader say what he or she means and support that with his or her actions? The answer to that question defines the soft skills of the leader.

The scenarios in this chapter are, in one way or another, related to a leader's Emotional Intelligence/Soft Skills. If your Leader Acumen assessment scores indicated this as an area for needed growth, you should work through the scenarios with a couple of things in mind. First, as you work through the scenarios in the chapter, take particular note of the *Contributing Authors' Options* to each problem at the end of each chapter of SJTs. In working through the scenarios and reviewing the *Contributing Authors' Options*, one of the two things will happen. You will find disparity between your responses and the authors, or you might, indeed, find that your responses coincide with the authors' (see Appendix B for a graphic representation). Next, reflect on the information you gained from the Leader Acumen assessment. If you acknowledge that Emotional Intelligence/Soft Skills is an area for growth based on the assessment, ask yourself if this was based on your Self assessment, the Circle assessment, or both.

If either or both assessments (the Self or Circle) indicate that you have room for improvement in the area of leader Emotional Intelligence/Soft Skills *and* you are also finding disparity in yours and the *Contributing Authors' Options*, chances are you will find growth via working through these exercises and accompanying readings. However, be reminded, this will not happen overnight. Growing your *Leader Acumen* is a worthy endeavor but is a painstakingly time-consuming undertaking. It requires rewiring of your thought processes regarding learnings that are very ingrained into your most innate understandings and this takes time (see Appendix B for a graphic representation).

On the other hand, if you find your solutions and the solutions offered in the *Contributing Authors' Options* coincide highly, yet your Self score is lower than the mean shown at the end of your Leader Acumen assessment for Emotional Intelligence/Soft Skills, one of the two things is happening. Either you are lacking in self-confidence, yet your decision-making is solid; or conversely, perhaps you are somewhat overconfident but nonetheless making good decisions. If the first is the case, working through the scenarios should enhance your self-confidence. The second option (overconfidence) is the one to be most wary of. Leaders in this category, many times, find themselves derailed as leaders, even though they generally are good decision makers. Working through the scenarios should help to instill the idea that there is more than one acceptable solution to most problem/issues and thus lessen one potential major consequence of overconfidence, feeling that you have the only viable solution.

If you opt to have a Circle/360 assessment done and find that your solutions and the solutions offered in the *Contributing Authors' Options* coincide highly, yet your Circle scores were outside the standard deviation (available from the LEAD team when a Circle/360 assessment is done) for Emotional Intelligence/Soft Skills, it is possible that a different set of problems is occurring. Either you are selecting the course of action you believe is best for the scenario, yet in reality you would not implement it, or the problem may be one of *perception*. It is much more likely that it is the former. Only in rare instances would the latter be the case. However, we insert it here for thought because, on occasion, it is the case. And, as the old saying goes, "Perception is reality."

Perhaps you have indeed highly honed soft skills, yet *perception* is the issue for your low scores in Emotional Intelligence/Soft Skills. This could be a case of projection. For example, you may not seem emotionally intelligent and perhaps for legitimate reasons. You will recall from the chapter on credibility in *The Soft Skills of Leadership: Navigating with Confidence and Humility*, mention was made of how "what you wear" infers or projects an image. Such could be the case in this instance.

Finally, improving your leader acumen and "adaptive capacity" as stated in the preface is a process. As you will recall, the notion of leader acumen is predicated on the theory that there is a genetic predisposition toward leadership.

As Marquis and Tilcsik[1] so aptly noted, imprinting may take place, during brief sensitive periods of high susceptibility during the formative process, during the teachable moment, or another yet different time of susceptibility; and that imprints once established are persistent. The lessons in this book are to be utilized to grow Leader Acumen in this third way—over the long, repetitive process. To that end and to truly be imprinted with any of the competencies, actions for building the various skill sets may be found in Appendix C.

> The leader who, through developing his/her leader acumen, can also master the ability to recognize and react appropriately to both the rational and emotional sides of an individual has a decided advantage over the leader who lacks those abilities.[2]

DEMONSTRATIONS AND RECRIMINATIONS

With a packed-to-capacity gym, the superintendent and high school principal enter for the biggest rival game of the season. As they enter, the national anthem begins to play, and from the corner of the superintendent's eye, he notices two of the basketball players take a knee. Within five minutes, the news has posted the demonstration online and the superintendent has gotten several texts from the media requesting a comment. The superintendent and principal formulate a response that appears to be well received and continue to watch the game while monitoring social media outlets.

Over the next two days, parents and alumni begin to make phone calls showing their disapproval of the demonstration. The superintendent meets with the students and coaches to discuss the event and to formulate plans for moving forward. Other demonstrations across the state are linked to the local demonstration, and students begin to be called names and threatened online. Rumors fly as parents begin taking their children off the team, business supporters begin withdrawing support, and threats to come on the sideline loom. Hearing all of this has raised safety concerns; therefore, the administration has made the decision to rearrange the pregame activities, keeping the players in the locker room during the national anthem for the duration of the season. A group of parents and concerned citizens contact a local attorney to begin proceedings against the district to force the district to keep demonstrating students in the locker room and allow all others on the sideline.

What do you do?

Suggested Reading: Maulding Green, W., and Leonard, E. (2019). *The Soft Skills of Leadership: Navigating with Confidence and Humility*, 2nd ed., Chapter 7. Lanham, MD: Rowman & Littlefield.

Additional Selected Reading: Trejo, A. (2016). "Project Outcomes Improved by Emotional Intelligence." *Business Perspectives & Research*, *4*(1), 67–76. doi:10.1177/2278533715605436.

FIRST MEETING DRAMA

The life of a leader can come with many rewarding experiences, but it also can be filled with many agonizing decisions that can leave one feeling emotionally and physically drained. Each day brings on new challenges, new decisions, many of which affect the livelihoods of the adults who serve in your system.

Dr. Benny Thomas, a former middle school principal in a neighboring district, has just been named the new principal of Riverside High School. Riverside High School has been one of the highest performing high schools in the state for the past several years, and the naming of the new principal has caused some angst among the staff. One of the former assistant principals was the staff's favorite to get the job, and now there is a clear divide that is causing many of the staff to take to social media and even protest to the board of education regarding their dislike for the new hire. Needless to say, the welcoming of the new principal was subpar at best.

Benny is not dismayed by all of the chaos surrounding his hire. He has been in education for over twenty years and truly understands the grieving process staff goes through when a principal retires after serving in that position for over fifteen years. His first day on the job has finally arrived, and his first faculty meeting is underway. As he walks into the room, several of his teachers get up and leave, including the assistant principal who was denied the job.

Dr. Thomas is faced with a huge dilemma, especially since this will be the first time he addresses his staff. His next steps will be crucial in setting the tone for the new school year.

How do you address your staff?

____

____

____

____

____

____

____

Suggested Reading: Maulding Green, W., and Leonard, E. (2019). *The Soft Skills of Leadership: Navigating with Confidence and Humility*, 2nd ed., Chapter 7. Lanham, MD: Rowman & Littlefield.

Additional Selected Reading: Kim, H., and Kim, T. (2017). "Emotional Intelligence and Transformational Leadership: A Review of Empirical Studies." *Human Resource Development Review*, *16*(4), 377–93. doi:10.1177/1534484317729262.

A BUS DRIVER'S QUANDARY

It is your first year as a principal, and a bus driver asks if she can speak to you after the morning announcements. Today is Friday and the day of the annual Spring Fling, which means an additional 1,000+ people on campus. It is obviously a very busy day, and you hesitate to take time to meet with the bus driver. After a brief mental debate, you escort the bus driver to your office in a frantic, hurried state of mind. The bus driver states that a kindergarten student reported that Susie, a first-grade student, asked the kindergarten student to lick her in her private area. Immediately, the spring fling takes a backseat. You ask the assistant principal to take over the outside activities, and you began investigating the allegation.

You request the bus video from the director of transportation. Next, you call the kindergarten student to the office, and she reiterates the same story she shared with the bus driver. She also shares that two other students heard the conversation, so you interview them as well. Since all of the stories seem to line up, you decide it is time to speak with Susie. You have the school counselor speak with Susie about the incident.

Susie confirms the reported conversation and shares several disturbing things with the counselor. She stops short of reporting abuse, but there are enough warning signs to proceed with contacting the authorities. Susie is sent back to her class to participate in the spring fling. You call mom and asked her to report to the school immediately. You do not share any specific details, just relay a sense of urgency. Mom is without a car and says she will be there as soon as she finds a ride.

A short time later, mom arrives accompanied by a male friend of the family. You ask the friend to have a seat in the front office and take mom to your office. You share the details about the bus incident as well as your suspicions that Susie is being sexually abused. Mom is understandably upset and immediately shares suspicions she has about a friend of the family. As it turns out, it is that same friend who is waiting in the front office. The mom immediately calls Susie's grandparents and requests that they come to the school.

What are your next steps?

____

____

____

____

____

____

____

Suggested Reading: Maulding Green, W., and Leonard, E. (2019). *The Soft Skills of Leadership: Navigating with Confidence and Humility*, 2nd ed., Chapter 7. Lanham, MD: Rowman & Littlefield.

Additional Selected Reading: Livesey, P. V. (2017). "Goleman-Boyatzis Model of Emotional Intelligence for Dealing with Problems in Project Management." *Construction Economics & Building*, *17*(1), 20–45. doi:10.5130/AJCEB.v17i1.5101.

PAYING THE PRICE

Occasionally talented students with great potential find themselves in positions where the actions they take have a devastating effect on their future. As principal of the alternative school in your district, you are meeting with a senior and his grandparents, who are his guardians. Late in the second semester, this student was involved in a fight on school grounds, which ultimately resulted in him being assigned to complete his senior year in an alternative setting. Through examination of his records and conversations with his base school teachers, you see a picture of a student who had an excellent school record prior to this incident: no major disciplinary problems (and few minor ones), excellent grades and ACT score, and was a promising young athlete on track for college.

During the conversation with him, the student admits his poor judgment in becoming involved in the fight. He shows understanding of the seriousness of the incident and states that he wants to complete his high school diploma work and move on to college in the fall. He has been awarded a scholarship based on his ACT score and an additional sports scholarship conditional upon May graduation so that he can attend summer training camp. However, a problem presents itself when his credits are examined. He has not taken the fine arts class required for graduation, and that class is not offered in the alternative setting in your district.

Given the situation, what course of action do you take?

Suggested Reading: Maulding Green, W., and Leonard, E. (2019). *The Soft Skills of Leadership: Navigating with Confidence and Humility*, 2nd ed., Chapter 7. Lanham, MD: Rowman & Littlefield.

Additional Selected Reading: Benjamin, B. (2018). "The Resurgence of Emotional Intelligence: Six Reasons Why EQ Matters More than Ever." *Leadership Excellence Essentials*, *35*(3), 21.

WELCOME TO AMERICA

Public schools are places where students and parents of all cultures and ethnicities should be made to feel welcome and valued. Great school leaders understand the importance of building trusting, positive relationships with the community members that they serve. Even so, occasionally issues come up, which require teachers and administrators to exercise good judgment and sensitivity with regard to cultural differences.

In a large suburban early childhood public school, children gather daily in the cafeteria for breakfast and lunch. The school works hard to help children learn how to utilize the salad bars to serve themselves a variety of healthy choices. Soft talking and socializing are allowed and encouraged, as the administration of this school values the friendships, social language, and enjoyment that young children gain from sharing meals together.

Parents and guests of the students are welcome to eat breakfast or lunch at any time with their children in order to foster positive community relationships and make mealtimes a pleasant experience for everyone.

Recently, a four-year-old child has enrolled in the school. The child is newly emigrated from another country and has not yet learned to speak English. His parents enlisted the aid of a bilingual family friend to help register the child for the school's preschool program.

On the first day of school, the student's mother joined him for lunch. The school staff was surprised when the mother spoon-fed her son his entire lunch. The next day, the child's mother returned at lunchtime and engaged in the same unusual behavior. As time went on, it became evident that the child was not gaining the skills of independence or language, which mealtimes can afford, and was socializing with no one but his own mother. Both mother and child seemed quite happy with the arrangement of daily spoon-feeding at lunchtime. However, the child's teacher and administrators knew that it was important for this student to learn to feed himself and socialize with his peers.

What do you do?

Suggested Reading: Maulding Green, W., and Leonard, E. (2019). *The Soft Skills of Leadership: Navigating with Confidence and Humility*, 2nd ed., Chapter 7. Lanham, MD: Rowman & Littlefield.

Additional Selected Reading: Leonard, Alisa. (2017). "Millennial Priorities: The Rise of Emotional Intelligence." Retrieved from https://www.levo.com/posts/millennial-priorities-the-rise-of-emotional-intelligence.

GONE TOO SOON

Teenage suicide unfortunately occurs too often in our society. Many changes occur during the teen years, both physiological and psychological. During this same span of time, teens must learn to make appropriate decisions that will impact their future. They learn to make these decisions in an environment that is both competitive and judgmental. Peers are not the only group that heightens the stress for teens, often parents and teachers by the very nature of pushing students to do the best create unnecessary anxiety.

At your high school, a very volatile student dies in a single-car accident. The student has been in trouble at school several times and the parents also related incidents of noncompliance and even running away for several days at a time. As the accident is investigated, it is discovered that a suicide probably occurred, and drugs were involved.

What do you do?

____

____

____

____

____

____

____

Suggested Reading: Maulding Green, W., and Leonard, E. (2019). *The Soft Skills of Leadership: Navigating with Confidence and Humility*, 2nd ed., Chapter 7. Lanham, MD: Rowman & Littlefield.

Additional Selected Reading: Dabke, D. (2016). "Impact of Leader's Emotional Intelligence and Transformational Behavior on Perceived Leadership Effectiveness: A Multiple Source View." *Business Perspectives & Research*, *4*(1), 27–40. doi:10.1177/2278533715605433.

BY POPULAR REQUEST

It is the end of the school year and you are getting a lot of parent notes requesting their child have the Teacher of the Year as their homeroom teacher next school year. At last count, you have over ninety parent letters requesting this teacher.

How will you respond to the requests?

Suggested Reading: Maulding Green, W., and Leonard, E. (2019). *The Soft Skills of Leadership: Navigating with Confidence and Humility*, 2nd ed., Chapter 7. Lanham, MD: Rowman & Littlefield.

Additional Selected Reading: Maddocks, J. (2017). "Does the Emotional Intelligence of Leaders Influence the Emotional Climate of the Organisation?" *Assessment & Development Matters*, *9*(3), 10–5.

BYE BYE BIRDIE

You are the principal of an elementary school in an elite area of town. Most of your teachers do not have a "needs list" because parents supply them with anything that is needed. Unfortunately, sometimes this causes parents to be demanding. One of your teachers has informed you that one of the very generous parents has expressed a concern over her child not passing the weekly spelling test. The teacher has met with the parents and suggested strategies for improvement. The parent declares that she will not be satisfied until her daughter does better.

Weeks go by, and the child is still underperforming. The parent shows up at central office with a demand that the class pet, a parakeet, is removed from the classroom. The parakeet that is loved by all the students and is the mascot for the class is now ousted by central office staff because of a possible allergy. This is the first that the teacher has heard of the allergy and believes that the removal of the pet is a power move from the parent. The teacher now wants the child removed from her room and wants to keep the parakeet unless the parent provides a note from a doctor.

What do you do as principal?

Suggested Reading: Maulding Green, W., and Leonard, E. (2019). *The Soft Skills of Leadership: Navigating with Confidence and Humility*, 2nd ed., Chapter 7. Lanham, MD: Rowman & Littlefield.

Additional Selected Reading: Jensen, D., and Bojeun, M. (2017). "The Value of Emotional Intelligence in Transformational Change." *AMA Quarterly*, *3*(1), 12–5.

10

CONTRIBUTING AUTHORS' OPTIONS FOR EMOTIONAL INTELLIGENCE SJTS

DEMONSTRATIONS AND RECRIMINATIONS

A. Allow the coach and the athletic director to handle the situation.
B. Ignore the situation; it will blow over in a few days.
C. Remove the athletes from the team as a disciplinary matter for the remainder of the school year.
D. Address the situation with the students, parents, and community with the principal, coach, and athletic director at your side.
E. Allow the team to go out while keeping the students who participated in the locker room during pregame rituals.
F. Another option:

____

____

____

FIRST MEETING DRAMA

A. Make a B-Line to retrieve the staff and assistant principal who have left the meeting.
B. Break the ice by telling a funny story.
C. Proceed with promoting your agenda for the new year.
D. Give the staff an opportunity to voice their concerns.
E. Communicate an action plan for uniting the staff and bringing the school together.

F. Another option:

____

____

____

A BUS DRIVER'S QUANDARY

A. Call the child welfare agency as any alleged abuse occurred off campus and they are the proper authorities to investigate the matter.
B. Call the police department as any alleged abuse occurred off campus and they are the proper authorities to investigate the matter.
C. Call the superintendent to inform her of the situation and to ask for advice.
D. Call the local prosecuting attorney as any alleged abuse occurred off campus and they are the proper authorities to investigate the matter.
E. Another option:

____

____

____

PAYING THE PRICE

A. Explain that an online version of the class is available, but the grandparents will have to pay the $250.00 tuition fee.
B. Explain that the mistakes that we make sometimes have unintended consequences. Since the class he needs is not offered in the alternative setting, it will be necessary to return to school the following year to complete the class.
C. Offer to allow the student to take the class during the summer session at a cost of $350.00, as per the current policy for summer coursework.
D. Explain that an online version of the class is available and can be paid for by the district in exchange for the student completing community service hours.
E. Another option:

____

____

____

WELCOME TO AMERICA

A. Schedule a meeting with the mother, the child's teachers, and a school interpreter familiar with the child's native culture to discuss the importance of helping the student build independence. Invite the mother to be a part of the process by allowing her to eat with her child and modeling for him how to serve himself and use his silverware.

B. Call the mother via an interpreter and ask her to refrain from visiting the school until her son develops the independence to feed himself during meals.

C. Allow the child and mother to eat in a different location in order to protect their privacy and avoid attracting attention from others.

D. No real harm or disruption is occurring. Just observe the child's social behaviors for the first year of his school career until his language skills become proficient enough to talk with him about how "big boys and girls" eat in the cafeteria.

E. Assign a willing peer buddy to eat with the child to help model appropriate behaviors.

F. Another option:

____

____

____

GONE TOO SOON

A. Let the parents handle the situation without assistance; pray and attend the funeral.

B. Prepare in advance for a catastrophic incident. Have a team in place that has been trained to ensure that student needs are met and decrease the likelihood that additional suicides occur because of the attention.

C. Try and get together a group of teachers to help with the students as quickly as possible.

D. Halt all school schedules and allow students to talk with each other throughout the day without adult supervision.

E. Ignore the incident.

F. Another option:

____

____

____

BY POPULAR REQUEST

A. Ignore the requests.

B. Accommodate the first thirty requests.

C. Ask for specifics from each of the parents why the request is necessary.

D. Send a newsletter home promoting all of your faculty and ask parents not to request specific teachers.
E. Another option:

____

____

____

BYE BYE BIRDIE

A. Remove the child from the classroom because she may be allergic to the bird.
B. Meet with the teacher and the parents to determine the real issues.
C. Ask the teacher to trade classroom pets with a teacher in the school for the remainder of the school year.
D. Visit central office and make a case for your teacher and the bird; if they say no, open the classroom window and let the bird go.
E. Another option:

____

____

____

CONTRIBUTING AUTHORS' SOLUTIONS FOR SJTS

Disclaimer: On the following pages are the author's recommended solutions, rationale, and reasoning for rejection of alternative solutions. These recommendations are in no way intended to supersede work policy or act as legal advice to the learner. These are actual situations encountered by the authors including the solutions they enacted at the time and place of the circumstance.

CONTRIBUTING AUTHORS' SOLUTIONS: CREDIBILITY

SO MANY PROBLEMS, SO LITTLE TIME

***Best Solution*:** C. Fulfill the commitment you made to the parent and take the time to call.

Rationale for Best Solution: Let your word be your bond. Relational trust is critical with parents, students, and staff. If you give your word, follow through. Problems do not tend to get smaller if ignored, if anything they tend to grow. When all else fails—keep your word. Even if you have to call and tell the parent the investigation will have to continue into the next week—you will have still kept your word by making that call. One final note: If it doesn't bother you if you don't make that call, you might be in the wrong line of work.

Rationale for Rejecting the Alternate Responses

A and D. Being busy is consistently the case for a school principal. Nonetheless, failure to follow-up/communicate in a timely manner will lead to a lack of parental trust and fails to address a potentially serious issue. This option is not a good choice.

B. If you have time to fully communicate the situation to the assistant principal, this option is viable but not the best option. If not, you are doing a disservice to all the parties involved.

SEARCHING FOR ANSWERS

***Best Solution*:** F. Contact the police and the parents of the student.

Rationale for Best Solution: Possession of drugs or drug paraphernalia (especially by minors) is a felony in most states. Therefore, the police should be involved and the student's parents notified.

Rationale for Rejecting the Alternate Responses

A, C, D. Parental notification is a good idea; the punishment, however, does not fit the offense.

B. Expulsion may be recommended but due process calls for smaller steps as a prelude.

E. Honesty is a worthy characteristic but leniency is not warranted given the offense.

PRINCIPLE I: SIMPLICITY

Best Solution: D. Wait out the situation and let the principal handle it when she returns.

Rationale for Best Solution: The twin girls are not in any danger at this point. You have checked the student's book bag and he does not have a weapon. The counselor has met with the student and the principal will return later during the day. In this type of situation, suspension will not change the student's behavior. The student needs true medical counseling if he is threatening to decapitate other students in their sleep. You know that what you were asked to do is unethical, therefore you allow the principal to handle the situation upon returning to work.

Rationale for Rejecting the Alternate Responses

A. This option could occur; however, it will reveal confidential notes from years of counseling.

B. This option could occur, but the child needs medical counseling attention over suspension.

C. This option should occur, but you should also stress the need for medical counseling.

THE DIGITAL AGE

Best Solution: C. Contact and meet with the parents to discuss the incident.

Rationale for Best Solution: As there was no direct threat to other students (by name) or school personnel, and the police have been made aware of the incident, meeting with the parents as formal notice from the school and to enlist their assistance is a proper first step.

Rationale for Rejecting the Alternate Responses

A. More action is required than noting the incident. Proactive prevention is needed.

B. As the police contact you, some discussion of appropriate action is warranted but more must be done than discussing the issue.

D. This is an avenue you should suggest to the parents and if informationally it will help you, then it should be done but it is a preliminary to taking action.
E. If a specific threat existed, this or more would be warranted.
F. If a specific threat existed, this or more would be warranted. However, this action could open the school to liability for psychiatric services.
G. The dual action suggested here is partly of questionable value (simply noting the incident) and partly highly valuable (garnering parental involvement/cooperation).

CHRISTMAS CHEER?

***Best Solution*:** B. Review the parents' divorce decree to confirm the father's legal status regarding his child and keep the child in school until the end of the day.
***Rationale for Best Solution*:** Even though the father was granted the right to have his son during the Christmas holidays that year, the holidays did not officially begin until the end of the school day. Keeping the son in school until the end of the school day was legally the correct decision to make.

Rationale for Rejecting the Alternate Solutions

A. Ensuring things are "right" by contacting the custodial parent is a possible solution; however, you may not be able to get in touch with the mother.
C. Notification to the superintendent is always a wise courtesy, especially in the event that the angry parent heads there next. However, the situation at hand must be properly dealt with first.
D. After notifying the noncustodial parent to wait until school dismissed, this is the next proper action to take in the event the parent creates additional problems.
D. Call the campus school resource officer (SRO) to have the father arrested for his threats and disruptive behavior.

SAFETY FIRST

***Best Solution*:** H. Immediately remove the student from class. Search for weapons.
***Rationale for Best Solution*:** The allegation that a weapon was/maybe on campus is enough to warrant removal of the student from class and a search. Caution and action when warranted are the watchwords for safety.

Rationale for Rejecting the Alternate Responses

A. To substantiate the allegations, this is a good step but not a needed first step.
B. This too is a good step but not the needed first step.

C. Making note of the incident is not sufficient as it leaves the door open for problems.
D. The police may become involved if a weapon is found but the advice of law enforcement is not needed initially.
E. This too is a good step but not the needed first step.
F. A suspension may be warranted if a weapon is found or the allegations substantiated but is not the needed first step.
G. This is an avenue you should suggest to the parents and if informationally it will help you, then it should be done but it is a preliminary to taking action.
I. If a specific threat is found to exist, this would be warranted. However, this action could open the school to liability for psychiatric services.
J. Expulsion may be recommended but due process calls for smaller steps as a prelude.

CONTRIBUTING AUTHORS' SOLUTIONS: COMPETENCE

CHANGING SCHOOL DYNAMICS

***Best Response*:** D. Provide guided PD with feedback to include strategies, language development, and cultural dynamics.

***Rationale for Best Solution*:** The key words to this PD option are guided with feedback. Plus, teachers need effective strategies that will help Hispanic students learn academic content, knowledge of language development to increase English language proficiency, and awareness of the cultural differences.

Rationale for Rejecting the Alternate Responses

A. This option does not provide any accountability that it will occur.
B. This option does not take into account the changing dynamics of the school plus needed differentiated strategies for the change.
C. This option should occur, although it is not the best option. This provides a scheduled time for the activity where some discussion may occur. The labels will help the Hispanic students learn the names of items in the school.
E. This is a good option to help teachers learn the language but it does not address Hispanic students learning academic content.

TO SERVE OR NOT TO SERVE

***Best Response*:** E. Although the school is not required to follow the psychometrist's diagnosis and recommendations, the report will initiate a discussion of the student's performance and determine the next steps. The process for the next steps will be discussed.

Rationale for Best Solution: The school is not required to follow the recommendations of an outside psychometrist. This report will initiate a discussion of the report and the results of the medication's effect on Kevin's performance and behavior. If Kevin is making the progress of an average student, then no formal plan is required (not required to provide the Cadillac version). In order to make sure Kevin's progress continues, the student will be monitored. If any issues arise, the school will discuss any next steps. The parents also need to be made aware of the 504 process—IDEA referral and 504 consideration if not IDEA eligible (IDEA Federal Law).

Rationale for Rejecting the Alternate Responses

A. A school is not required to follow the report of a psychometrist if done outside the school.

B. This should be done as good practice to help the teacher understand the ADHD disorder and how to provide typical accommodations.

C. Peer support can be done to a limited degree because peer students need to keep up with their own work and assignments.

D. The parents need to be made aware of the process that schools must follow based on federal requirements.

TO ERR IS HUMAN

Best Response: D. You correct the mistakes in class in a very professional manner making sure you do not embarrass the teacher.

Rationale for Best Solution: The evaluator should ask the teacher if he could show the kids an alternate solution method and model this method to the class. The teacher may then continue with the lesson and the incorrect solution can be addressed at a post-conference meeting.

Rationale for Rejecting the Alternate Responses

A. If you do not say anything, you leave the children with the impression that the incorrect method is correct.

B. Same as A.

C. Same as A and B above.

MEET THE PRESS

Situation A

***Best Response*:** D. Address the reporter and ask what her intentions are so that you can establish guidelines.

***Rationale for Best Solution*:** The administrator should approach the reporter, introduce him/herself, and ask what her intentions are regarding the situation.

Rationale for Rejecting the Alternate Responses

B. Asking the reporter to leave may inflame the situation and/or give the appearance of trying to hide something.

C. The reporter has not acted in a manner that warrants police involvement.

Situation B

***Best Response*:** C. Call the police and have her escorted off campus.

***Rationale for Best Solution*:** The parent obviously does not know how to behave properly on campus. Allow the authorities to do their jobs.

Rationale for Rejecting the Alternate Responses

A. She has no authority to be checking students out of school.

B. Explain to her that she cannot talk to other students and that she must leave campus.

D. Tell her she must wait until school is over to talk to students.

Author's Note: The administrator called the police and had the parent removed from campus since she was causing disruption and endangering the safety of other children. Parent (X) got a lawyer and a lawsuit was threatened but never moved past a general inquiry to receive information. The school has multiple pages of documentation regarding false claims by parent (X). Several of her neighbors came to the school to write statements in support of the school and to state that the child of parent (X) was actually the aggressor in the entire situation.

IT'S LONELY AT THE TOP

***Best Solution*:** B. You put the safety of your students and staff first. Err on the side of caution and wait for the roads to clear.

***Rationale for Best Solution*:** The safety of your students and staff should always be your number one goal. Relative to Maslow's Hierarchy of Needs—if the safety needs of your students and staff are not met, odds are very little that learning will take place anyway!

Rationale for Rejecting the Alternate Responses

A. You cannot be concerned with what other districts do is irrelevant. State testing is vitally important but more important than safety.
C. When balanced against student achievement, safety comes first. It is better to show the patience needed to insure the safety of the students and faculty/staff.
D. Some decisions should not be delegated. This is one of those. It is wise to seek the transportation director's advice but he or she should not make the final decision.

LITTLE MISS SUNSHINE

***Best Solution*:** B. Check with the school nurse to see if the child has a medical issue.
***Rationale for Best Solution*:** Unless there is some reason other than discomfort (getting hot and sweating), her seat should not be changed. The school nurse should be able to tell you or find out if the child has some condition that would warrant a seat change.

Rationale for Rejecting the Alternate Solutions

A. Ignoring the request could lead to further issues. It is better to deal with the issue and move on.
C. This solution is tempting and the driver may be involved in the eventual solution but the decision should be yours as principal.
D. This question will probably be taken as sarcasm by the parent, creating a trust issue.

CHARMIN SOFT?

***Best Solution*:** D. Ask the parent to purchase biodegradable/flushable baby wipes that can be flushed.
***Rationale for Best Solution*:** Using biodegradable/flushable wipes is a good solution for not only this child but all of the children or parents who would prefer wipes. The additional expense to the parent is minimal.

Rationale for Rejecting the Alternate Solutions

A. Throwing soiled wipes in the trash is a health hazard and should not be encouraged.
B. This is a good talking point to sell the idea of biodegradable/flushable wipes but is not the best solution.
C. While it is possible, if a medical condition mandated the use of wipes, it is unlikely to appear in the IEP. Still, checking never hurt but would be only one step toward a solution.

UNABLE TO WALK THE LINE

Best Solution: A. Call the local authorities or school police force and have them give the teacher a sobriety test.
Rationale for Best Solution: This action settles the question as to whether he is intoxicated.

Rationale for Rejecting the Alternate Solutions

B. If he is called into the office and his already defensive, there is no telling what could happen, so no to B.
C. Even though it would be unsafe for him to be on the road, it's not a good idea to try to block him in, so no to C.

Bloody Mess—Part I
Best Solution: Preferred Order E, A, B, D, F, C, G
Bloody Mess—Part II
Best Solution: Preferred Order A, E, C, D, F, B

CONTRIBUTING AUTHORS' SOLUTIONS: ABILITY TO INSPIRE

CRUNCH TIME

Best Solution: C. Reduce salaries of all employees in the district in order to meet the required cut and maintain the current number of teachers and support personnel.

Rationale for Best Solution: A salary cut (starting with the superintendent) for all employees shows that everyone in the district is in this together and it strengthens the commitment of the school district with the community by showing the personnel are willing to make less money while still providing the same quality service to the children of the county.

Rationale for Rejecting the Alternate Responses

A. While this accomplishes the goal of cutting the budget, it directly negatively impacts instruction, the local economy, and the individual employees.

B. While this too accomplishes the goal of cutting the budget, it jeopardizes the financial stability of the district and only postpones the decision.

D. Tax increases can be used to offset loss of state revenue but can never recoup entire state cuts. A tax increase and the other cuts are stopgap measures at best. A tax increase has the added negative effect of public dislike of tax increases. And, according to the present millage rate there, a tax increase may not be an option if the school district is already at or close to the cap.

ONE FOR THE ROAD?

***Best Solution*:** C. Call the resource officer and the child welfare agency as action by both may be needed.

***Rationale for Best Solution*:** Focus on the safety of the child by blocking her mother from taking the child while simultaneously seeking assistance for the child.

Rationale for Rejecting the Alternate Solutions

A. A good first step but incomplete in providing for the safety of the child.
B. Also a good first step but incomplete in providing for the safety of the child.
D. Calling to inform is warranted and for advice if unsure, but with other help already summoned this may delay needed action.

Author Note: The school resource officer, who was on loan from the local city police department, arrived and took over the situation. Katie's mom was arrested for public intoxication and possession of an illegal substance and removed from campus. Katie's grandmother was contacted and arrived a few minutes later. The child welfare agency developed a care plan on-site and awarded guardianship to the grandmother.

This incident occurred during my first semester as an elementary principal. There was no guideline or set of procedures for this particular situation. I simply focused on Katie's safety and shielding her from the situation as much as possible. As a follow-up to the scenario, three months later custody was returned to the parent by the child welfare agency, which found no evidence of neglect or endangerment.

KEEPING YOUR PROMISE

***Best Solution*:** E. Conduct a full investigation upon your return, and then take appropriate disciplinary action.

Rationale for Best Solution: All students should be afforded due process rights prior to taking serious disciplinary actions. The public expects speed and accuracy in these situations. Getting it right the first time will avoid negative publicity due to impulsiveness.

Rationale for Rejecting the Alternate Solutions

A. Referring the matter to law enforcement for further investigation is a possibility. Assistance may be required, but this is not the best option.
B. Going on vacation (avoidance) will not make things better.
C. Immediately suspend all students involved, pending expulsion. This is an option but requires further investigation.

D. Direct your assistant principal to handle the matter. This is an option but not the best for this scenario.

DOMESTIC VIOLENCE—PART I

Best Solution: A. Call the police and support her as she files a police report.

Rationale for Best Solution: If she is willing to file for a protective order or actual charges, the man can be put on notice and/or arrested for his behavior. It is a first step in protecting her and her children.

Rational for Rejecting the Alternate Solutions

B. While this is a compassionate thing to offer and provides immediate safety, it does not begin the process needed for her and her children's long-term security.

C. A bad idea as he is already mad at her.

D. A worthwhile approach but one that shunts the immediate problem away from you and the support you can provide.

DOMESTIC VIOLENCE—PART II

Best Solution: C. Call the police and school system resource officer.

Rationale for Best Solution: The police in cooperation with the school resource officer can act against the man both in the community and at the school if needed.

Rational for Rejecting the Alternate Solutions

A. Keeping the school on lockdown helps to avert an immediate threat but cannot be sustained without affecting the entire school population.

B. The teacher should be apprised of the situation for her own protection but should not be discouraged from coming to work.

D. Hiring extra security is not needed if the police and campus resource officer work in concert.

POPULAR REQUEST OF A DIFFERENT KIND

Best Solution: B. Meet with each parent individually asking for specific reasons for the request moving students.

***Rationale for Best Solution*:** Teacher loads must be balanced and on the whole, she is a good teacher. The parents need to know that you believe in her. Your belief will positively impact the parents.

Rationale for Rejecting the Alternate Solutions

A. This may be the eventual answer for many but should not be the starting point.
C. This should have already happened and definitely needs to happen but is not the solution to the immediate issue.
D. Changing all the schedules will not work as you involve more parents with more opinions to deal with.

A PROM DILEMMA

***Best Solution*:** D. Let the election run its course. If the elected Prom Queen refuses to dance with the elected Prom King for the traditional "First Dance," then continue the evening without a "First Dance."
***Rationale for Best Solution*:** Having allowed the election to move forward and if the outcome is as you predict, simply announce and crown the King and Queen and start the prom without the traditional "First Dance." Thus, you are honoring the rights (one to her or his identity and the other the right to refuse to dance with someone of the same sex) of all while minimally departing from tradition.

A. A tempting solution but one that fails to address the equality and justice issues involved.
B. Obviously a "tongue in cheek" response but not an acceptable response.
C. Another tempting solution but stubbornly moving forward will create an untenable situation for you, the school, and school district.

CONTRIBUTING AUTHORS' SOLUTIONS: VISION

DROPPING AN "F" BOMB

***Best Solution*:** D. Meet with the teacher to discuss the allegations.

Rationale for Best Solution: Without direct observation, meeting with the teacher is the professional thing to do. It allows the teacher the opportunity to deny or admit to the actions alleged while simultaneously allowing you to take action based on the teacher's response.

Rationale for Rejecting the Alternate Responses

A. The likelihood of there being a repetition of the behavior in your presence as principal is negligible. However, unannounced drop-in observations are one means of insuring that teachers stay on task. That makes this option somewhat good.
B. It is unprofessional to divulge alleged inappropriate teacher behavior to other teachers.
C. It is unprofessional to discuss alleged inappropriate teacher behavior with parents.
E. Ignoring students, unless there is substantial basis for doing so, undermines your credibility as principal.

SCHOOL IS NEVER BORING

***Best solution*:** B. Apologize to the parent who complained, declare two winners, and award the student who was disqualified a first-place ribbon along with the student who was awarded the blue ribbon when the first student was disqualified.

***Rationale for Best Solution*:** In this case, the error was on the part of the administration because a complete investigation was not done before a decision was made. We explained to the student why his board was disqualified and also why he was receiving a first-place ribbon. Encourage him to follow all guidelines in the future and commend him for being honest.*

Rationale for Rejecting the Alternate Solutions

A. Starting over penalizes everyone and causes more difficulties.
C. Asking for further guidance is acceptable but places the burden of decision on the superintendent who obviously does not want to be involved.
D. This decision satisfies no one as it penalizes those who were told they had won or finished high enough to receive a ribbon.

INSUBORDINATION?

Best Solution: A. You present your view to the teacher and work to reach a compromise.

***Rationale for Best Solution*:** There are obviously some issues on both sides. On the leader's side, the teacher has ignored a directive and in becoming defensive and accusatory has reached a point of insubordination when she says she will continue to ignore the directive. On the teacher's side, there is frustration regarding assistance with classroom discipline and with the directive that appears to go counter to her teaching beliefs. Airing of differences by both parties is the first step in coming to a resolution.

Rationale for Rejecting the Alternate Responses

B. Meeting with the leadership team, depending on who is on the team, may be a good idea but in general is counterintuitive as the team will not have to make the decision as to what actions to take moving forward.
C. It is unprofessional to discuss teacher professional/personnel issues with parents.
D. As with the best solution, a cooling-off period is often advisable. However, given the teacher's declaration about ignoring the directive, more immediate action is required.
E. Acting to terminate, given the teacher's stance regarding the directive, is tempting but the end result may negatively impact students. Arriving at a compromise is a better solution.

WHERE DO WE GO FROM HERE?

Best Solution: E. Survey students to determine if changed criteria would create enough interest to fully populate the advanced classes. Survey the teachers to determine if they would be willing to teach an extra prep to keep the advanced classes. Work with the community college to establish a relationship to offer the classes.

Rationale for Best Solution: The discovery that the minimum requirements for the class had been incorrectly applied was actually a "blessing in disguise." Under the right conditions (as happened in this actual scenario—see next), lemonade can be made out of lemons!

Rationale for Rejecting the Alternate Solutions

A. With reduced funding, adjustments must be made. This might be the last option but should not be the first option.
B. This would surely end the classes resulting in a net loss for all concerned.
C. This represents dual enrollment and might be a viable alternative but is not a first step.
D. Offering the classes every other year could be a viable option if the "best solution" had not worked out.

Author's Note: A survey was done with students to see if the criteria changed would there be enough interest to fully populate the advanced classes. The teachers were also surveyed to determine if a teacher would be willing to teach an extra prep to keep the advanced classes. The students were eager to take the classes and were willing to accept the challenge of a more rigorous class, especially for college credit as well as high school. Teachers with a master's degree were willing to teach an extra prep and allowed the students to have a class that counted as dual enrollment. The community college was also willing to send a teacher to teach that class if the secondary teacher did not have the appropriate certification. Enough students enrolled in the advanced classes that the number of students in the regular classes was reduced and one teacher was able to handle the teaching load that had taken two because of the low numbers in the advanced classes. Additional benefits included the building of the relationship between the secondary school and the community college so that even more classes could be offered at the secondary school using community college faculty for one or two periods.

JUST KID'S PLAY?

Best Solution: C. Provide a mandatory daycare after school with supervision on-site at a low cost. D. Reprimand the teacher for calling parents and discipline the students for fighting on campus.

***Rationale for Best Solution*:** The teacher acted inappropriately and warranted a reprimand. Both students were at fault and deserved to be disciplined. Looking ahead and being concerned for the safety of students in the future (having seen that it was unsafe for students to be unsupervised) moving forward, teachers' children will need to attend the after-school daycare if staying on campus after the school day.

Rationale for Rejecting the Alternate Solutions

A. While this is a tempting solution, there is already animosity between the two. Left alone rather than solving the problem may exacerbate it.
B. All of the teachers were not involved. Group punishment for individual offenses is counterproductive.

ABOUT THAT MOVE

***Best Solution*:** D. Inform board members of the situation and proceed as planned.
***Rationale for Best Solution*:** Discussions on the redistricting plan have been in progress for the past few years. Finding a way to keep the district out of dire financial straits is imperative. Declining enrollment is a major cost-prohibiting factor.

Rationale for Rejecting the Alternate Solutions

A. Delaying the vote will cost the district additional monies.
B. The vote needs to take place. Not hearing additional input avoids the situation.
C. This further delays the decision. This is not the best option.
E. Revamping the plan is not an option at this point in time.

CONTRIBUTING AUTHORS' SOLUTIONS: EMOTIONAL INTELLIGENCE/SOFT SKILLS

DEMONSTRATIONS AND RECRIMINATIONS

Best Solution (*For this situation in the location*)**:** D. Address the situation with all stakeholders with the principal, coach, and athletic director at your side.

***Rationale for Best Solution*:** The situation had gotten statewide publicity and was beginning to get out of control. Clear and direct expectations for the public and community needed to be addressed by the superintendent.

Rationale for Rejecting the Alternate Responses

A. The situation had gotten too big to be handled at the school level.
B. The situation had made statewide news outlets and was being shared and attached to other schools who were beginning to have similar demonstrations.
C. The students had a constitutional right to peaceful protest whether administrators agree with the how and when.
E. This level of isolation would not allow the students to exercise their constitutional rights; either they all go out or all stay in.

FIRST MEETING DRAMA

***Best Solution*:** E. Communicate an action plan for uniting the staff and bringing the school together.

Rationale for Best Solution: With so much tension and anxiety existing among the staff, it is imperative that you take this opportunity to unite the staff. Starting your first faculty meeting off in a negative way would add more fuel to the fire, and this will be the first opportunity for you as the leader to truly lead by example, to be the change that you want to see in your staff.

Rationale for Rejecting the Alternate Solutions

A. If they have chosen to leave the meeting, they expressed their concerns publicly. Let that stand as their statement. Deal with them privately and move on in a positive manner.
B. There are times for levity. This is not one of them.
C. This will need to be done but is not the needed first step.
D. This will need to be done but is best done one-on-one to avoid divisiveness.

Author's Note: Dr. Smith has quite the mountain in front of him. Not only does he have staff that are not interested in giving him a chance, one of his assistant principals carries the same sentiments. With any change, there always will be some dislike and you will *never* have 100 percent buy-in. Before you can push your agenda as a new administrator, you first must build relationships and communicate a plan for uniting staff. Trying to do anything before this will be disastrous. Even though you did not chase after those that left, you must have a conversation with them. You must approach this meeting with loving intentions and really listen intently as to the real reason they are upset. It could be that they are nervous about the change, or anticipating major changes affecting their jobs, or it could be a cultural thing that may just take time to heal. Regardless of the reason, that conversation with each of those individuals who left the meeting is paramount. It would be a wise idea to set up a listen and learn opportunity with the staff to gain insight into their concerns and ideas around keeping the high achievement moving forward. Transparency is also key to follow-up with your staff regarding the ideas they had regarding ways to move forward. It's very strategic to include some of your most vocal staff on committees like a principal advisory or school cabinet team. The best way to handle your naysayers is to involve them in the process. Outside of addressing your staff, there is some work to be done around building trust among your administrative team. Having a one-on-one discussion with them is also crucial, because if your administrative team is dysfunctional it will breed dysfunction throughout your building. This scenario captures the true essence of leadership. It requires humility, vulnerability, thoughtful action steps, boldness and it most certainly leaves pride and egos at the door.

A BUS DRIVER'S QUANDARY

Best Solution: B. Call the police department as any alleged abused occurred off campus and they are the proper authorities to investigate the matter.

Rationale for Best Solution: As the allegations are very serious but occurred off campus, the local police have jurisdiction and the expertise to carry out the needed follow-up investigation.

Rationale for Rejecting the Alternate Solutions

A. A good first step but incomplete in providing for the safety of the child.
C. Calling to inform is warranted and for advice, if unsure, but with other help already summoned this may delay needed action.
D. The prosecuting attorney may be involved if the police find evidence to substantiate the alleged abuse but a first call is unwarranted

Author's Note: About this time, around six detectives from the sex crimes division of the local police department arrived on campus. I found a private area away from the mom and family friend and shared the situation with them. The detectives proceeded to interview the mom in my office. The family friend was moved to a conference room and interviewed. Once the grandmother and husband arrived on campus, emotions and tempers were running high and there was an emotional scene in the front office.

The police were able to get the family friend off campus without a physical altercation with Susie's dad or grandmother. Susie and her family went to the police station to complete the process of pressing charges. Susie also received counseling from a local child abuse agency. As I reflected on the incident, I realized the importance of taking time to listen and being flexible. I never made it to the spring fling that day, or finished anything else on my to-do list for the day, but I learned an important lesson about prioritizing and valuing the input from all staff members.

PAYING THE PRICE

Best Solution: D. Explain that an online version of the class is available and can be paid for by the district in exchange for the student completing community service hours.

Rationale for Best Solution: Explain that an online version of the class is available and can be paid for by the district in exchange for the student completing community service hours.

Rationale for Rejecting Alternate Responses

A. The online class will fill the need for earning the credit needed to graduate but may put a financial burden on grandparents living on a fixed income. Building community relationships between parents and school often requires that administrators go beyond the quick solution to seek out the best solution.

B. Don't throw the baby out with the bathwater. Although students must and should be held accountable for their actions, uncaring decisions that fail to seek creative solutions often fail to meet the ultimate needs of the student's future.

C. This solution still falls short of "best practice" leaving fixed-income grandparents with a heavy burden, a student with no "buy-in" to a solution, and a later graduation date that may cost him scholarship dollars.

WELCOME TO AMERICA

Best Solution: A. Schedule a meeting with the mother, the child's teachers, and a school interpreter familiar with the child's native culture to discuss the importance of helping the student build independence. Invite the mother to be a part of the process by allowing her to eat with her child and modeling for him how to serve himself and use his silverware.

Rationale for Best Solution: This young child has not been given the opportunity to gain independence or socialize with his peers during mealtimes. In his native culture, it may be acceptable for his mother to spoon-feed him; however, an important part of a quality early childhood education includes helping children gain self-help skills, social skills, and language. A friendly conversation from this point of view can foster an understanding on the part of the parent. By engaging her in the plan to help her child achieve social and self-help skills in the cafeteria, we can help her to feel valued as an important member of the school community and include her in the process of helping her child grow in confidence. Bringing in a knowledgeable interpreter from the school is important to foster understanding and gives the mother a resource for future school communication needs, which builds trust.

Rationale for Rejecting the Alternate Responses

B. Although the child is not proficient in English, allowing the spoon-feeding behavior to occur at school will not foster the student's self-help skills or social skills, nor will it foster a healthy relationship between the mother and the adults who work with her child.

C. The mother's presence is not causing a disruptive environment for the school. There is no reason to ask the mother to refrain from visiting the school if other parents are allowed to eat with their children, and it could be interpreted as discrimination. It is appropriate to work with her in partnership to help her child to develop age-appropriate self-help skills.

D. Parents and children are part of the school community, and every effort must be made to make them feel welcome and valued. Allowing a child to withdraw from his or her peers will not foster social skills, language acquisition, or age-appropriate behaviors.

E. This should also occur but it alone does not address the source of the concern.

GONE TOO SOON

Best Solution: B. Prepare in advance for a catastrophic incident. Have a team in place that has been trained to ensure that student needs are met and decrease the likelihood that additional suicides occur because of the attention.

Rationale for Best Solution: The school had set up a group of community members that include clergy and counselors as well as parents and others who have been trained to assist in the school with the grieving process should a catastrophic incident occur. The school counselors immediately contacted this team to be on-site at the school throughout the day following the incident. During homeroom period, the students could sign up for a time to meet with a community member if needed. The community members talked with the students in small groups or individually and encouraged them to begin the grieving process. In addition, the community team met with the school counselor and other school personnel to ensure that students who needed additional follow-up could have that option. The school tried to maintain the schedule for the day to create a normal atmosphere and a sense of security while respecting the student's needs.

Rationale for Rejecting the Alternate Solutions

A. This is often done, especially, and pays due respect to the parents who have suffered the loss but leaves the school population dealing with their needs alone.

C. Teachers are always willing to help but can often be as overcome as the students. A possible solution, if other resources are not available.

D. Staying with the routine is often the best, and adult supervision is always required in a school setting.

E. Ignoring the incident is the worst solution as it shows a lack of respect for the student, parents, and the general school and community population.

BY POPULAR REQUEST

Best Solution: D. Send a newsletter home promoting all of your faculty and ask parents not to request specific teachers.

Rationale for Best Solution: Each teacher is valuable to the success of the school; your belief in them impacts the perception of the parents.

Rationale for Rejecting the Alternate Solutions

A. Ignoring the parents only prolongs the problem. If they cannot get satisfaction from you, they will probably go over your head.
B. Even if this were done first come, first served and is practiced for all teachers, it would not resolve the problem. And, first come, first served puts some parents (those who cannot easily come forward) at an immediate disadvantage.
C. Each parent will present the best case they can. And having made their case each will expect to be accommodated while in the end the decision will still be arbitrary. This is a sure way to anger parents.

BYE BYE BIRDIE

***Best Solution*:** B. Meet with the teacher and the parents to determine the real issues.
Rational for Best Solution: Yes—you need to meet with both teacher and parents and get to the real issues. Also, if she is truly allergic, then C, ask the teacher to trade pets with another class for the remainder of the year.

Rationale for Rejecting the Alternate Solutions

A. Can't remove the child because she has friends in the class, and it would be unfair to her.
C. This could be done as a viable alternative if warranted but is not a good first step.
D. Going to central office without speaking to the parent first would be a bad idea.

APPENDIX A

SMALL GROUP CARDS

(Cut out individual letters and laminate for class use)

A	B
C	D
E	F

APPENDIX B

LEADER ACUMEN INTERPRETATION CHART

When reviewing your Self/Circle graph, keep in mind that there can be four outcomes for each of the five skill sets as well as your total Leader Acumen score. Begin by considering your Total score; then, move to your category of greatest relative weakness. Remember, a strength overused can become a liability.

*Leader Acumen Self/Circle Assessment Matrix**

High Self/High Circle *Most Desirable Orientation* *Strong in category and strong Self/Circle congruence suggests that Leadership Orientation is well developed and recognized.* *Skill enhancement is advisable for continued success.*	**Low Self/High Circle** *A Problematic Orientation* (Preferred over a High Self/Low Circle orientation) *Low Self scores and high Circle scores indicate a Leadership Orientation lacking in leader self-confidence.* *Leader growth is needed although the Circle has confidence in the leader.*
High Self/Low Circle *A Problematic Orientation* *Leadership Potential for Egocentric/Narcissistic Orientation* *Weak Circle congruence suggests a need for leader growth and development of the Leader–Circle relationship.* *Without growth derailment is likely.*	**Low Self/Low Circle** *Least Desirable Orientation* *Orientation with most room for growth.* *Though there may be congruence between the Self and Circle scores in this orientation, this Leadership orientation suggests a need for leader growth and development of the Leader–Circle relationship focused on success.*

* The Self and Circle scores, as well as congruence of the Self and Circle scores, vary along a spectrum from low to high. For each scenario, the Authors' Choices are typical of high Self/high Circle responses. This matrix represents the most likely outcomes and orientations.

APPENDIX C

LEADERSHIP ORIENTATION

Being perceived as and feeling individually that you are competent is vital to leader success. To this end, higher education leaders, like competent leaders in all fields, impact the perceptions of others by the way they behave/act/speak. Those behaviors/acts/utterances exemplify/personify the leader's level of competence to organizational members and constituents. But how can a leader gain insight or come to understand how he or she is perceived? One way to gain such insight into or understanding of how he or she is perceived is through 360-evaluative feedback.

In combination with that feedback, it is vital that a leader individually be consistently reflective personally and professionally. That reflective process allows a leader to understand who they are and what they stand for as a leader and defines his or her leadership competence. That competence is one characteristic that tends to set them apart as a leader—to give them discernibility. And competence is often the key to both long-term and short-term success as a leader.

A list of characteristics often associated with effective leadership in higher education is provided below. Rate each item below on a scale of 1 to 10 (with 1 being lowest in importance and 10 being highest in importance) in relation to the item's importance in displaying leadership competence. A scoring rubric is provided in Appendix D.

1	Establish principles of treating people	1	2	3	4	5	6	7	8	9	10
2	Foster collaboration	1	2	3	4	5	6	7	8	9	10
3	Seek opportunities to make changes	1	2	3	4	5	6	7	8	9	10
4	Envision the future with a unique image	1	2	3	4	5	6	7	8	9	10
5	Keep hope and determination alive	1	2	3	4	5	6	7	8	9	10
6	Experiment and take risks	1	2	3	4	5	6	7	8	9	10
7	Set standards of excellence	1	2	3	4	5	6	7	8	9	10

8	Get people to see exciting possibilities	1	2	3	4	5	6	7	8	9	10
9	Recognize individuals' contributions	1	2	3	4	5	6	7	8	9	10
10	Build team spirit	1	2	3	4	5	6	7	8	9	10
11	Breathe life into the (organizational) vision	1	2	3	4	5	6	7	8	9	10
12	Share rewards within the team	1	2	3	4	5	6	7	8	9	10
13	Actively involve others	1	2	3	4	5	6	7	8	9	10
14	Create opportunities for success	1	2	3	4	5	6	7	8	9	10
15	Accept mistakes, disappointments, and failures as opportunities to learn.	1	2	3	4	5	6	7	8	9	10

Table based on the work of Simon Black.[1]

Enter your rating for each item below and in the scoring rubric for Leadership Orientation below.

1 ____	2 ____	3 ____	4 ____	5 ____
6 ____	7 ____	8 ____	9 ____	10 ____
11 ____	12 ____	13 ____	14 ____	15 ____

Categories based on the work of Simon Black.[2]

Scoring: Models the Way = sum items 1, 7, and 14

____ + ____ + ____ = ____________________

1 7 14 Models the Way total score

Inspire a Shared Vision = sum items 4, 8, and 11

____ + ____ + ____ = ____________________

4 8 11 Inspire a Shared Vision total score

Challenge the Process = sum items 3, 6, and 15

____ + ____ + ____ = ____________________

3 6 15 Challenge the Process total score

Enable others to Act = sum items 2, 10, and 13

____ + ____ + ____ = ____________________

2 10 13 Enable Others to Act total score

Encourage the Heart = sum items 5, 9, and 12

____ + ____ + ____ = ____________________

5 9 12 Encourage the Heart total score

Interpretation: The scores represent your emphasis of a given orientation as a higher education leader. The higher the score, the more prominent that orientation emphasis is likely to be in your leadership activities.

APPENDIX D

FUN AT WORK

Happiness is a highly individualized and internalized feeling both personally and professionally. While for purposes of discussion, personal and professional happiness can be separated, the two often carry over and impact each other. Still, being happy in our personal lives does not guarantee happiness in our professional lives nor does the opposite apply.

Beyond whatever carryover exists, a leader has minimal opportunities to impact the personal happiness of organizational members. Conversely, there are things a leader can do to increase potential professional happiness.

Rate each item below on a scale of 1 to 10 (with 1 being the lowest importance and 10 being the highest importance) in relation to the item's importance in promoting organizational members professional happiness. A scoring rubric is provided below.

A	Encourage organizational members to offer praise when accomplishments are achieved	1	2	3	4	5	6	7	8	9	10
B	Provide access to high-quality training and professional growth opportunities	1	2	3	4	5	6	7	8	9	10
C	At appropriate times, encourage staff members to take earned time off	1	2	3	4	5	6	7	8	9	10
D	Display energy and enthusiasm in working with organizational members	1	2	3	4	5	6	7	8	9	10
E	Insure that pay and benefits are competitive, fair, equal for equal work, and maximized	1	2	3	4	5	6	7	8	9	10
F	Be cordial and friendly	1	2	3	4	5	6	7	8	9	10
G	Provide organizational members opportunities for decision-making discretion (Porath et al., 2012)	1	2	3	4	5	6	7	8	9	10

H	Offer to mentor aspiring leaders	1	2	3	4	5	6	7	8	9	10
I	Provide feedback about performance (Porath et al., 2012)	1	2	3	4	5	6	7	8	9	10
J	Have and share an optimistic outlook as a leader	1	2	3	4	5	6	7	8	9	10
K	Provide equal access to opportunities for promotion	1	2	3	4	5	6	7	8	9	10
L	Deflect praise for successes to the responsible organizational members	1	2	3	4	5	6	7	8	9	10

Scoring: egocentric = sum items D, F, H, and J

____ + ____ + ____ + ____ = ________________

D F H J total egocentric score

people-oriented = sum items A, C, E, and L

____ + ____ + ____ + ____ = ________________

A C E L total people-oriented score

task-oriented = sum items B, G, I, and K

____ + ____ + ____ + ____ = ________________

B G I K total task-oriented score

Interpretation: The scores represent your tendencies toward behaviors that promote organizational member professional happiness. The higher the score, the more prominent this orientation is likely to be in your leadership activities. The maximum score for each category is 40.

BACKGROUND

Professional satisfaction/happiness has been shown to be related to worker performance. Therefore, incorporating those behaviors in a leader's repertoire of behaviors enhances the probability of worker satisfaction/happiness and organizational productivity.

"The Importance of Happiness in the Workplace." (2012). *Leader to Leader*, *63*, 62–3. doi:10.1002/ltl.20012.

Porath, C., Spreitzer, G., Gibson, C., and Garnett, F. G. (2012). "Thriving at Work: Toward Its Measurement, Construct Validation, and Theoretical Refinement." *Journal of Organizational Behavior*, *33*(2), 250–75. doi:10.1002/job.756.

Kerns, C. D. (2008). "Putting Performance and Happiness Together in the Workplace." *Graziado Business Review*, *1*(1). Retrieved from http://gbr.pepperdine.edu/2010/08/putting-performance-and-happiness-together-in-the-workplace/.

APPENDIX E

SELF-KNOWLEDGE

Warren Bennis (2002), well-known author and leadership expert says of leaders, "The ruling quality of leaders, adaptive capacity, is what allows true leaders to make the nimble decisions that bring success. Adaptive capacity is also what allows some people to transcend the setbacks and losses that come with age and to reinvent themselves again and again."[1]

Bennis' notion of adaptive capacity can be viewed as an applied amalgamation of the personality traits espoused in the five-factor model of personality. McCrae and John (1992) in describing the five-factor model held that there are "five basic dimensions: Extraversion, Agreeableness, Conscientiousness, Neuroticism, and Openness to Experience."[2] Neuroticism, in this instance, can be further defined as emotional stability.

1. Read each item carefully.
2. Select the answer that best describes how often you engage in the behavior described: (A) Always, (B) Often, (C) Occasionally, (D) Seldom, or (E) Never.
3. Circle the letter (A B C D E) of the answer you select.

A scoring rubric is provided in the Authors' Options section at the end of the chapter.

Item #	*Item*	*Always*	*Often*	*Occasionally*	*Seldom*	*Never*
A	I like to join multiple groups/ organizations	A	B	C	D	E
B	I consider myself imaginative in my approach tasks	A	B	C	D	E
C	I am even-tempered	A	B	C	D	E
D	I am hardworking	A	B	C	D	E
E	I am generally good-natured	A	B	C	D	E

Item #	Item	Always	Often	Occasionally	Seldom	Never
F	I am comfortable personally and professionally	A	B	C	D	E
G	I have a strong sense of curiosity	A	B	C	D	E
H	I am punctual	A	B	C	D	E
I	I tend to be forgiving of mistakes	A	B	C	D	E
J	I remain calm in most situations	A	B	C	D	E
K	I am active physically and mentally	A	B	C	D	E
L	I seek new approaches	A	B	C	D	E
M	I am trusting of others	A	B	C	D	E
N	I am highly verbal	A	B	C	D	E
O	I am well organized	A	B	C	D	E

BACKGROUND

The five-factor model of personality has been shown to be related to a variety factors that contribute to leadership success such as job satisfaction (Judge, Heller, and Mount, 2002), life satisfaction (DeNeve and Cooper, 1998), organization citizenship (Chiaburu et al., 2011), and work environment (Ruth, 2016). Aspects of the model, specifically, extraversion and agreeableness, have been shown to be positively related to transformational leadership (Judge and Bono, 2000).

Judge, T. A., Heller, D., and Mount, M. K. (2002). "Five-Factor Model of Personality and Job Satisfaction: A Meta-Analysis." *Journal of Applied Psychology*, *87*(3), 530–41. doi:10.1037/0021-9010.87.3.530.

DeNeve, K. M., and Cooper, H. (1998). "The Happy Personality: A Meta-Analysis of 137 Personality Traits and Subjective Well-Being." *Psychological Bulletin*, (2), 197.

Chiaburu, D. S., Oh, I., Berry, C. M., Li, N., and Gardner, R. G. (2011). "The Five-Factor Model of Personality Traits and Organizational Citizenship Behaviors: A Meta-Analysis." *Journal of Applied Psychology*, *96*(6), 1140–66. doi:10.1037/a0024004.

Ruth, J. A. (2016). "An Examination of the Impact of the Big Five Personality Traits and Work Environment on the Leadership Behaviors of Millennial Generation Employees." *Dissertation Abstracts International Section A*, *76*, 129–199.

Judge, T. A., and Bono, J. E. (2000). "Five-Factor Model of Personality and Transformational Leadership." *Journal of Applied Psychology*, *85*(5), 751–65. doi:10.1037/0021-9010.85.5.751.

SELF-KNOWLEDGE

Item #	Item	Always	Often	Occasionally	Seldom	Never
1	I like to join multiple groups/ organizations	A	B	C	D	E
2	I consider myself imaginative in my approach tasks	A	B	C	D	E

Item #	Item	Always	Often	Occasionally	Seldom	Never
3	I am is even-tempered	A	B	C	D	E
4	I am hardworking	A	B	C	D	E
5	I am generally good-natured	A	B	C	D	E
6	I am comfortable personally and professionally	A	B	C	D	E
7	I have a strong sense of curiosity	A	B	C	D	E
8	I am punctual	A	B	C	D	E
9	I tend to be forgiving of mistakes	A	B	C	D	E
10	I remain calm in most situations	A	B	C	D	E
11	I am active physically and mentally	A	B	C	D	E
12	I seek new approaches	A	B	C	D	E
13	I am trusting of others	A	B	C	D	E
14	I am highly verbal	A	B	C	D	E
15	I am well organized	A	B	C	D	E

Bennis, W. G. (2004). "The Seven Ages of the Leader." *Harvard Business Review*, *82*(1), 46.

McCrae, R. R., and John, O. P. (1992). "An Introduction to the Five-Factor Model and Its Applications." *Journal of Personality*, *60*(2), 175–215.

Scale items based on the "Examples of Adjectives, Q-Sort Items, and Questionnaire Scales Defining the Five Factors" (McRae and John, 1992, pp. 178–79).

SCORING

For the letter selected for each item, give yourself the following points. Then, total the scores for each category.

A = 5   B = 4   C = 3   D = 2   E = 1

				Total
1. Extraversion	1__	11__	14__	(____)
2. Agreeableness	5__	9__	13__	(____)
3. Conscientiousness	4__	8__	15__	(____)
4. Neuroticism (emotional stability)	3__	6__	10__	(____)
5. Openness to experience	2__	7__	12__	(____)

INTERPRETATION

The wide acceptance of the five-factor model and the extensive research indicating the relationship of the model's factors to leadership and life success make it essential that leaders understand their personality tendencies and dispositions. The results of this scale indicate your self-perception in relation to the aspects of the five-factor model. A higher score in a given area indicates that your personality tends to reflect characteristics of that factor.

BACKGROUND

The five-factor model of personality has been shown to be related to a variety factors that contribute to leadership success such as job satisfaction (Judge, Heller, and Mount, 2002), life satisfaction (DeNeve and Cooper, 1998), organization citizenship (Chiaburu et al., 2011), and work environment (Ruth, 2016). Aspects of the model, specifically, extraversion and agreeableness, have been shown to be directly positively related to transformational leadership (Judge and Bono, 2000).

Judge, T. A., and Bono, J. E. (2000). "Five-Factor Model of Personality and Transformational Leadership." *Journal of Applied Psychology*, *85*(5), 751–65. doi:10.1037/0021-9010.85.5.751.

Judge, T. A., Heller, D., and Mount, M. K. (2002). "Five-Factor Model of Personality and Job Satisfaction: A Meta-Analysis." *Journal of Applied Psychology*, *87*(3), 530–41. doi:10.1037/0021-9010.87.3.530.

Chiaburu, D. S., Oh, I., Berry, C. M., Li, N., and Gardner, R. G. (2011). "The Five-Factor Model of Personality Traits and Organizational Citizenship Behaviors: A Meta-Analysis." *Journal of Applied Psychology*, *96*(6), 1140–66. doi:10.1037/a0024004.

DeNeve, K. M., and Cooper, H. (1998). "The Happy Personality: A Meta-Analysis of 137 Personality Traits and Subjective Well-Being." *Psychological Bulletin*, (2), 197.

Ruth, J. A. (2016). "An Examination of the Impact of the Big Five Personality Traits and Work Environment on the Leadership Behaviors of Millennial Generation Employees." *Dissertation Abstracts International Section A*, *76*.

APPENDIX F

ACTIVITIES TO IMPROVE YOUR LEADER ACUMEN

Now is a good time to reflect on the navigational analysis. Let's consider that you are the driver for a chartered bus with thirty-five travelers to a landmark tourist adventure 600 miles away. You have made many trips over your life that were 600 miles or longer, but perhaps you have never been to this particular destination. Maybe some of those on the bus are older than you are and have driven longer. Perhaps, even, some of them have been to the destination at hand on a previous occasion. Prior to embarking on the trip, you have several options in preparation for the trip.

Regardless of how you chose to prepare, each of your travelers has his or her own expectations regarding the trip. Some may wish you would drive faste; others might wish you would have taken the more leisurely scenic route. Still others may question the detours, pit stops, and even announcements you make. All of these factors (and many others) would inform their feedback on your performance as a driver.

After returning from your destination and having a little time to reflect on the trip, you, too, might consider different decisions you would make if you had the chance to "drive the bus again." Your own reflections as well as the passenger's feedback would certainly leave an imprint. How strong an imprint might depend on the degree of congruence between your perception of the trip and theirs?

In order to improve the next trip (and not to imply that this one was a bad one), the driver needs to be reflective, ask for feedback, and plan for the future. This planning (for improvement) could include a myriad of things from using a more updated map (or GPS) to planning to take the trip at a better time of year. It will include both study and action.

The same planning for improvement, study, and action is true with *Leader Acumen*. The scenarios in the field book are given to help the leader consider the myriad of solutions to different problems and to become more effective and efficient at resolving them. Whether in a group setting with the rich dialogue, discourse, and reflective dynamics that setting generates or considered individually, study leading to action will be the best teacher and provide a clear/direct route to success in increasing your *Leader Acumen*.

As the leader becomes aware of and chooses the construct or skill set (Credibility, Competence, Inspiration, Vision, or Emotional Intelligence) he or she would most likely to improve, along with the exercises in the book, the following activities are recommended. For the best results, these activities should be planned and acted upon over a period of not less than six months.

To improve your Credibility, while working through the book scenarios, as odd as it may seem, write an article or research paper for publication to share your experiences and expertise. This is *not* a one-week assignment. You should set aside (at a minimum) weekly time to work on the article or paper: organizing, researching, and writing the article or paper. This won't just be for the sake of obtaining facts and information, it will also be for the purpose of presenting them. How you present yourself in your writing is a huge part of your credibility.

If you rush through and/or are sloppy, you leave a distinctly poor impression with the reader (think e-mails, memoranda, and even handwritten notes). As a leader, in any written correspondence, if you give the facts and figures without ensuring they are valid, reliable, and in fact real, again, you lose credibility. As you are preparing your paper, work to triangulate (using multiple data sources) to ensure your credibility. A second option would be to undertake case study readings about historical or contemporary figures you admire and believe to be credible and reflect on what about that individual/those individuals made them credible. These case studies could also be incorporated into your article or research paper.

To improve your Competence, while working through the book scenarios, align yourself with a mentor in your field of leadership and meet with him or her regularly. Try to find opportunities not only to interact with this person on an informal basis but more importantly find opportunities to "shadow" this person. Write down a list of questions to ask about how he or she arrived at a specific solution or why he or she took a certain position. Take the time to discuss with your mentor other solutions he or she (or you) might have considered. Talk to this person about typical problems/issues they encounter and how they approach resolving those problems/issues. Spend as much time talking about the why as the what, how, and about the timing of their decisions. Don't be timid when asking about technical matters. Technical matters form the basis, the what, people are to accomplish.

To improve your Ability to Inspire Others, while working through the book scenarios, join a speaker's bureau. Or, conversely, become a coach/sponsor/leader for a children's athletic, drama, music, or scout group. You might rather choose to join adult groups such as a neighborhood watch, owners' association, or civic group such as Rotary or Lions where you would have the opportunity lead by your words and actions.

As a member of a speakers' group, seek opportunities to present motivational/inspirational messages regularly. The same is true if you choose to become a volunteer coach/sponsor/leader of children's groups. Be sure that you give motivational pitches regularly to the children. With adults, volunteer to lead or participate in group activities. Being actively involved in the suggested activities should present ample opportunities to both observe and be a part of inspirational activities and should have a corresponding positive impact on your overall ability in this area.

To improve your Vision, while working through the book scenarios, embark on a personal improvement plan. This can be anything from a physical, spiritual, mental, or emotional area of your life. This idea is to choose an area for self-improvement and then to map out a six-month plan to reach a specific goal. As Covey would say, "Begin with the end in mind."[1] Once you have created the plan, and make it very detailed and specific, enact the plan. At the end of each month, evaluate and reflect on your progress and then adjust your plan accordingly. Or, as an alternative strategy, plan an event or series of events for your family or other group with which you are associated. Be sure to engage family or group members in the planning processes to produce a shared vision regarding each event. The personal plan or the planning of events should engage you actively in the give and take of reaching a personal decision that impacts your individual plan (or the consensus) that is needed for visionary action.

To improve your Emotional Intelligence/Soft Skills, while working through the book scenarios, commit yourself to involvement with a charitable, civic, school, religious, or other worthwhile organization that is not a part of your work. Focus your energies not only on the betterment of the cause/organization but specifically on the people affiliated with the cause/organization. Be intentional in your desire to encourage, support, and embolden them. Or, as an alternative strategy, volunteer to assist in projects sponsored by local civic groups that involve working with people in need or volunteer to work in an appropriate capacity at a hospital or nursing home or to assist youth groups in your community. The emotional impact of serving others selflessly should provide opportunities for growth in your emotional intelligence.

The combination of intense review of SJTs along with the activities as briefly described above over a period of time will ensure growth in your chosen *Leader Acumen* skill set. Not only will your skill set scores improve but, more importantly, your leadership capacity will improve. Your road to success as a leader will be like an up-to-date GPS with all the latest features, newest maps, and best route guidance available.

NOTES

PREFACE

1. Wanda S. Maulding Green and Edward E. Leonard. (2019). *The Soft Skills of Leadership: Navigating with Confidence and Humility* (Lanham, MD: Rowman & Littlefield).

2. Warren G. Bennis and Robert Thomas. (2002). *Geeks and Geezers: How Era, Values, and Defining Moments Shape Leaders* (Boston, MA: Harvard Business School).

3. Ibid.

4. Warren G. Bennis. (2004). "The Seven Ages of the Leader." *Harvard Business Review*, *82*(1), 46.

5. Chambers, J. (2016). "Cisco's John Chambers on the Digital Era." Retrieved from http://www.mckinsey.com/industries/high-tech/our-insights/ciscosjohn-chambers-on-the-digital-era.

6. M. Uhl-Bien and M. Arena. (2018). "Leadership for Organizational Adaptability: A Theoretical Synthesis and Integrative Framework." *The Leadership Quarterly*, *29*(1), 89–104. https://doi-org.lynx.lib.usm.edu/10.1016/j.leaqua.2017.12.009.

INTRODUCTION

1. Green and Leonard, *The Soft Skills of Leadership*.

2. Ibid., p. 19.

* Disclaimer: At the end of the book are the contributing author's recommended solutions, rationale, and reasoning for rejection of alternative solutions. These recommendations are in no way intended to supersede work policy or act as legal advice to the learner. If encountering similar situations, you should consult with proper authorities and/or act as you deem appropriate based on your own judgment. The Situational Judgement Test (SJT) scenarios included are based on actual situations encountered by the contributing authors including the solutions

they enacted at the time and place of the circumstance and may or may not be appropriate today individually or in your place of work.

SITUATIONAL JUDGMENT TESTS

1. Michael McDaniel and Deborah Whetzel. (2005). "Situational Judgement Tests." Lecture, IPMAAC Workshop, June 20, 2005.
2. Michael McDaniel, Frederick Morgeson, Elizabeth Finnigan, and Michael Campion. (2001). "Use of Situational Judgment Tests to Predict Job Performance: A Clarification of the Literature." *Journal of Applied Psychology*, *84*(4), 730–40.

CHAPTER 1

1. Christopher Marquis and Andras Tilcsik. (2013). "Imprinting: Toward a Multilevel Theory." *Academy of Management Annals*, 7(1), 195–245.

CHAPTER 3

1. Ibid.
2. Green and Leonard, *The Soft Skills of Leadership*.

CHAPTER 5

1. Marquis and Tilcsik, "Imprinting."
2. Green and Leonard, *The Soft Skills of Leadership*.

CHAPTER 7

1. Marquis and Tilcsik, "Imprinting."
2. Green and Leonard, *The Soft Skills of Leadership*.

CHAPTER 9

1. Marquis and Tilcsik, "Imprinting."
2. Green and Leonard, *The Soft Skills of Leadership*.

APPENDIX C

1. Simon A. Black, "Qualities of Effective Leadership in Higher Education," *Open Journal of Leadership* 4(2) (2015): 54–66. Retrieved October 15, 2016 from http://file.scirp.org/Html/2-233 0076_57195.htm.
2. Ibid.

APPENDIX E

1. Warren G. Bennis. (2004). "The Seven Ages of the Leader." *Harvard Business Review 82*(1), 46.
2. Robert R. McCrae and Oliver P. John. (1992). "An Introduction to the Five-Factor Model and Its Applications." *Journal of Personality, 60*(2), 175–215.

APPENDIX F

1. Covey, S. (1989). *The Seven Habits of Highly Effective People: Restoring the Character Ethic : 7 Habits of Highly Effective People* (New York: Simon & Schuster).

ABOUT THE AUTHORS

Wanda S. Maulding Green is an educational leadership faculty member at the University of South Alabama and has served in leadership roles in both K–12 and higher education. She is coauthor of the book, *Leadership Intelligence: Navigating to Your True North.*

Edward E. Leonard is a retired school superintendent and higher education administrator. He currently teaches leadership courses at the University of South Alabama and is coauthor of the book, *Leadership Intelligence: Navigating to Your True North.*

ABOUT THE CONTRIBUTORS

Dr. Sharon Bradberry served as an educator for thirty-five years prior to retiring. She held positions as an elementary and special education teacher, special education administrator, and elementary principal in Texas. She currently devotes her time to genealogy and lineage organizations.

Kathy Bunyard is a retired educator who during her career taught ungraded K-3, pre-K, special education, kindergarten, and ended her career as Curriculum/Federal Programs Director for the Forest Municipal School District, which she faithfully served for thirty-one years. Additionally, she was instrumental in the development of the EL and the pre-K programs.

Dr. Ben Burnett is the dean of the School of Education at William Carey University. His service to the field of education began in 1986 and since that time he has worked with the students of Mississippi as a band director, middle school principal, superintendent of education, and dean.

Phyllis P. Campbell recently retired with thirty-five years of service all with the Forest Municipal School District. During those years, she served as a classroom teacher as well as assistant principal at Forest Elementary, principal at Hawkins Middle School, and retired as the special education director with the district. She currently serves as a consultant with The Excellence Group.

Joe Carpenter has been an educator and school administrator for over twenty-one years. He is currently employed with the Baldwin County School District at Gulf Shores High School as an assistant principal. He enjoys boating, fishing, and spending time at the beach with his family.

Dr. Courtney Diaz is currently an assistant principal for the Mobile County Public School System. She is also an Educational Leadership adjunct professor in the Leadership and Teacher Education Department at the University of South Alabama.

Dr. Carla J. Evers is superintendent of the Pass Christian School District. The district was recently featured in ASCD's Disrupting Poverty series and has been recognized as one of the top-rated school districts in the state. In the past decade, the district was ranked first in the state for five consecutive years. Under her leadership, the district continues to be an A-Level district.

Dr. Brian Finnigan is currently a principal at Saraland Alternative Learning School in Saraland, Alabama. He formerly served as an assistant principal and science teacher for seventeen years. Prior to his work in education, Dr. Finnigan held leadership roles as a chemical production manager for fifteen years and seven years as a research chemist.

Dr. Timothy Holland is the principal at Long Beach Middle School. He is a former math teacher and baseball coach. Dr. Holland received his degrees from the University of Mississippi, William Carey University, and the University of Southern Mississippi.

Dr. B. R. Jones has over twenty years of experience in K–12 education. He currently is the principal at Jones County School District in Ellisville, Mississippi, and is the author of *The Focus Model: Systematic School Improvement for all Schools.*

Michele McClung is currently Director of Curriculum, Instruction, and Assessment of a large school district in the southeast. She has served as a teacher, curriculum supervisor, assistant principal, and principal for twenty-eight years.

Dr. Cindy Morgan has served as a teacher, counselor, and assistant superintendent. She has taught foundation classes for Educational Leadership at the University of Mississippi and served as a research professor at Mississippi State University. She is currently co-owner of The Excellence Group, LLC.

Dr. Patricia Permenter is a retired Mississippi educator and assistant professor at William Carey University. She also serves as the associate director of Program of Research and Evaluation for Public Schools (PREPS).

Mrs. Nilene Quave is a retired educator who invested thirty-five years in expanding the minds and hearts of students. She taught in both Mississippi and Alabama schools in both elementary and middle school classrooms. She also spent ten years as administrator in both the middle school and the alternative school settings.

Anthony Sampson is the Director of Prevention and Support Systems for Baldwin County Schools in South Alabama. Sampson has a history of work experience in K–12 that includes career development, event planning, and coaching. He is the proud father of three beautiful children.

Dr. Jessica Stubbs is currently the principal of the 3-D School Gulf Coast Campus, a special-purpose school for children with dyslexia. She has served as a kindergarten teacher, an early childhood instructional coach, and is a strong community advocate for families impacted by dyslexia.

Dr. Christopher J. Williams, Sr., is currently the assistant superintendent in Ocean Springs School District, where he oversees K–12 Curriculum, Federal Programs, District Testing, and supervises principals. He received his Ph.D. from the University of Southern Mississippi. He is the father of two children, Christopher, Jr., age nine and Jade, age seven, and has been married to Dr. Jamie L. Williams for thirteen years.

Dr. Kimberly Williams is currently an elementary school principal in Saraland City Schools and is an adjunct instructor at the University of Mobile. She has served as a kindergarten teacher, third-grade teacher, reading specialist, K–12 instructional specialist, and an assistant principal.